Type Recipes

Quick Solutions to Designing with Type

Designed and Written
by Gregory Wolfe
in collaboration
with Viva Goorian

NORTH
LIGHT
BOOKS

Cincinnati, Ohio

Type Recipes

Copyright © 1991 by Gregory Wolfe.
Printed and bound in the United States of
America. All rights reserved. No part of this
book may be reproduced in any form or by
any electronic or mechanical means including information storage and retrieval
systems without permission in writing from
the publisher, except by a reviewer, who
may quote brief passages in a review.
Published by North Light Books, an imprint
of F&W Publications, Inc., 1507 Dana Avenue, Cincinnati, Ohio 45207. First edition.

95 94 93 92 91   5 4 3 2 1

**Library of Congress Cataloging in
Publication Data**

Wolfe, Gregory
    Type recipes / Gregory Wolfe.—1st ed.
        p.   cm.
    ISBN 0-89134-393-8 (pbk.)
    1. Printing, Practical—Layout.
    2. Printing, Practical—Style manuals.
    3. Type and type-founding. I. Title.
    Z246.W65 1991
    686.2'1—dc20   91-17683
                                         CIP

Edited by Diana Martin and Dawn Korth
Interior designed by Gregory Wolfe

In the type samples, pages 26–125 of this
book, any similarity to actual people, companies, logotypes or situations is strictly
coincidental.

For our loving parents,
Roger and Mary Wolfe,
and Leonard and Myrrl Goorian

About The Author

Gregory Wolfe was educated at the Kansas City Art Institute and Indiana University in Bloomington. He has taught at the Herron School of Art IUPUI, Kansas City Art Institute, Indiana University and the University of Cincinnati. He currently teaches typography and graphic design and conducts research in computer graphics at the Art Academy of Cincinnati, where he has chaired the Communication Design Program. He writes software reviews on type and graphics programs for *HOW* magazine. His designs have been exhibited by the International Typographic Composition Association, *Print* and *IDEA*. He is creative director for Gregory Wolfe Associates, Inc. in Morrow, Ohio.

Contents

Ten of the most popular and flexible typefaces are shown:

- in a full range of available styles including light, text, bold, extra bold, condensed, expanded, italic and oblique
- with horizontal scaling of standard type styles to create special and unique effects
- using a variety of letter, word and line spacings for impact

Discover how to work successfully with:

Part 2: Type Moods and Design Options

A buffet of 300 typographic design options at your fingertips lets you choose the typeface and specifications that will create the ideal mood to successfully communicate **any** message.

Whether you are designing a logo for a nostalgic neighborhood restaurant, a traditional letterhead for an attorney, or a sign for a trendy boutique, you'll find your just-right solution in these mood categories.

Part 3: The Idea Collection

Discover even more ideas and inspiration for using type to create perfect moods with ads, newsletters, business cards, magazines, logos, business forms, newspapers and promotional materials featured here.

Appendix

Introduction

Type Recipes presents a rational approach to selecting type styles by illustrating and explaining how to use type to fit the mood you want to express. I have provided the type basics for using the most popular type styles and shown examples of how to use them effectively to create a mood. Ideas used to solve type problems in this book may be very similar to problems you encounter with your work. Many of the technical tips will provide a helpful head start for art directing or hands-on production.

This book is written for desktop publishers, graphic designers, writers or anyone who is producing typeset printed materials. Understanding how to create type moods gives you the power to produce persuasive printed messages.

Typographic problems are different from those of a decade ago. Not only has the technology changed, but the responsibility for producing printed communications has also. Traditionally writers worked with graphic designers, who in turn worked with typesetting companies to produce type. Now many graphic designers and writers are working with computers to produce typeset products. In other words, the personal computer may have placed the responsibility of producing end-product typography in your hands. The technical information included in this book can serve as a daily reference guide for selecting, specifying and creating custom typographic effects.

All of the logos and applications presented here are electronically generated and computer manipulated. Each example includes a technical brief on the process used to create the image. These illustrations will increase your understanding and stimulate ideas about moods and the processes used to create them. Understanding how to create effective typographic moods for a variety of clients employing a limited collection of type fonts is challenging. Remember that the effect is only as strong as the idea behind it. Tools create great effects in the hands of imaginative writers and graphic designers.

By using the technical specifications provided, you can duplicate the ideas using whatever mechanical processes you are familiar with. You may also use the book to show someone else the effects you want to create. The *Type Recipes* are specifications that can be re-created to fit your needs or simply serve as food for thought.

About the Book

This book will help you select type to create a mood. The three parts of this book should be used as a guide for making technical and aesthetic judgments about creating moods with typography. The first section presents ten type families that can be used to create different typographic moods. The second part explores the moods created by each of the ten type families presented in the first section. The third part of the book presents a collection of quality examples that show how other professionals have used type to creatively solve graphic design problems.

Type Styles and Special Effects

This section discusses how to identify, select, specify, produce, and create type effects using ten different type families. There are examples of the best type sizes, spacing and line lengths for you to use. Using the exact specifications right out of the book will help you produce successful typography the first time. When you want to create your own oblique, condensed or expanded type style you'll save time by selecting one of the samples and modifying it to meet your own needs.

The examples used in this section are based on accepted typographic rules and traditional standards.

Type Moods

Each of the ten moods is produced with a single type family and electronic variations of that family. Each mood works with five different companies to illustrate how you can use the same type family to create a similar mood for *different* kinds of clients. A selection of logos, as well as practical applications such as business cards, letterheads, envelopes, signs and ads represent a variety of typographic styles and effects for each company. In many instances the same logo is reproduced in different moods with only the type style changed. As you study the business applications, look for how symmetrical and asymmetrical composition also affects the moods.

The Idea Collection

This section shows examples of good typographic design. You can see how professionals use type to create moods. You will also notice how the use of photography and illustration greatly enhance the effectiveness of the mood.

Characteristics

Avant Garde has the appearance of a mechanically constructed geometric type design, but it has many subtle refinements that prove otherwise when you inspect individual characters. Avant Garde has a smooth look that was produced by careful hand-drawn refinement of each letter. The vertical strokes and the diagonals are not the same weights, and circular strokes also have subtle changes in weight. The capital *Q* and *R* and lowercase *g* are distinctive characters that will help you identify the family characteristics. These refinements distinguish Avant Garde from earlier geometric type styles such as Futura and Tempo. The x-height is very high in Avant Garde; consequently there is little distinction between the capitals and lowercase letters. The short ascenders and descenders reduce the readability of this face, particularly in smaller sizes. Avant Garde is a trendy typeface that will produce a contemporary look in product logos, trade show displays and advertising graphics.

Type styles:

Book

Book Oblique

Demi

Demi Oblique

Type style: Book. Size: 48 points.

ABCDEFGHIJKL
MNOPQRSTUV
WXYZabcdefgh
ijklmnopqrstuvw
xyz12345&6789

Tracking. Type style: Book. Size: 10 points.

Tracking adjusts interletter and interword spacing. Very tight (-%₂₀₀ em)

Tracking adjusts interletter and interword spacing. Tight (-%₂₀₀ em)

Tracking adjusts interletter and interword spacing. Normal

Tracking adjusts interletter and interword spacing. Loose (+%₂₀₀ em)

Tracking adjusts interletter and interword spacing. Very loose (+%₂₀₀ em)

Tips

- Avant Garde's interword and interletter space can be set from normal to very tight.
- Set text in sizes 10 points and larger to improve readability.
- Use larger point sizes when you print on uncoated paper stocks to compensate for the texture of the paper.
- When setting justified text try using extra interline space to improve readability.

- Use 140 percent of the point size of the letter as normal interline space. This compensates for the extremely high x-height.
- Display sizes are particularly adaptable to the tight overlapping of letters, called "knit" typography in advertising.
- Using a modified horizontal scale to expand Avant Garde is visually acceptable to 350 percent.

- Avoid excessively condensing Avant Garde in text applications. The vertical strokes become thin and distorted.
- Generally use Avant Garde for fashionable applications in advertising, packaging and displays.
- Avant Garde is also excellent for trendy packaging and display applications.
- Mood reference: see Trendy, pages 26-35.

Type style: Book. Alignment: Flush left/ragged right. Size: 10 points. Interline space: 14 points. Tracking: Normal. Line length: 19 picas.

Interline spacing is used to separate individual lines of type from each other. The visual space between lines should be greater than the interword space. Generous interline spacing ensures that the reader will be able to scan each line of the text without interruption.

Type style: Demi. Alignment: Flush left/ragged right. Size: 10 points. Interline space: 14 points. Tracking: Normal. Line length: 19 picas.

Interline spacing is used to separate individual lines of type from each other. The visual space between lines should be greater than the interword space. Generous interline spacing ensures that the reader will be able to scan each line of the text without interruption.

Type style: Book. Alignment: Justified. Size: 10 points. Interline space: 14 points. Tracking: Normal. Line length: 19 picas.

Interline spacing is used to separate individual lines of type from each other. The visual space between lines should be greater than the interword space. Generous interline spacing ensures that the reader will be able to scan each line of the text without interruption.

Type style: Book. Size: 18 points. Tracking: Normal. Horizontal scale: 85%.

Type style: Book. Size: 18 points. Tracking: -9/200 em. Horizontal scale: 150%.

Type style: Book. Size: 18 points. Tracking: -9/200 em. Horizontal scale: 350%.

Type style: Book. Size: 18 points. Tracking: -13/200 em. Horizontal scale: 150%.

Type style: Demi. Size: 18 points. Tracking: -18/200 em. Horizontal scale: 350%.

Type style: Book Oblique. Size: 18 points. Tracking: -9/200 em. Horizontal scale: 300%.

Type style: Demi Oblique. Size: 18 points. Tracking: -9/200 em. Horizontal scale: 300%.

Characteristics

The Bodoni type styles reflect the eighteenth-century art of engraving popular during the industrial revolution. The fine detail of the Bodoni design would have been impossible to print with earlier printing presses and rough pressed paper stocks. Bodoni still favors open letterspacing even though the type style has been re-proportioned for use on today's typesetting machines. The italic type styles are carefully constructed but reminiscent of pen-and-ink letters. The extreme thin strokes and the hairline serifs, frequently without brackets, combine to create a delightful regular rhythm. The slightly condensed proportions of the capitals will save a considerable amount of space if you're setting headlines in all caps. Bodoni has a short x-height and can be set with little or no interline space, but it must be set in larger sizes. The Bold and Black Condensed have a higher x-height that requires more interline space, but they can be set in smaller sizes. The Bodoni family is available in a good selection of type styles from the standard Bodoni to the decorative heavyweight Poster design.

Type styles:

Bodoni

Italic

Bold

Bold Italic

Bold Condensed

Black Condensed

Black

Black Italic

Poster

Type style: Bodoni. Size: 48 points

ABCDEFGHIJK
LMNOPQRSTU
VWXYZabcdefg
hijklmnopqrstuv
wxyz12345&678

Tracking. Type style: Bodoni. Size: 12 points

Tracking adjusts interletter and interword spacing. Very tight (-5/200 em)

Tracking adjusts interletter and interword spacing. Tight (-4/200 em)

Tracking adjusts interletter and interword spacing. Normal

Tracking adjusts interletter and interword spacing. Loose (+4/200 em)

Tracking adjusts interletter and interword spacing. Very loose (+5/200 em)

Tips

- Bodoni is a romantic specialty typeface that should not be used in situations requiring large amounts of text.
- Set in sizes 12 points or larger because of the short x-height and thin strokes.
- Use larger sizes for applications printed on uncoated paper.
- Avoid printing Bodoni text on gloss coated stock; it produces a visual vibration.
- Use a loose rag or centered text without hyphenation and a 20 pica line length.
- Avoid any tight kerning. Use normal to plus tracking when setting Bodoni text.
- Large headlines can be tightly tracked and carefully kerned to produce striking results.
- Bodoni works with nongeometric sans serif type such as Helvetica, but avoid mixing with other serif faces or sans serifs such as Avant Garde.
- Poster is easily modified for use as an oblique style, horizontally condensed or expanded to extremes.
- This is definitely a specialized typeface for nostalgic advertising, fashion and brochures and posters.
- Mood reference: see Nostalgic, pages 36-45.

Type style: Bodoni. Alignment: Flush left/ragged right without hyphenation. Size: 12 points. Interline space: 14 points. Tracking: Normal. Line length: 21 picas.

Interline spacing is used to separate individual lines of type from each other. The visual space between lines should be greater than the interword space. Generous interline spacing ensures that the reader will be able to scan each line of the text without interruption.

Type style: Bodoni Bold Condensed. Alignment: Flush left/ragged right without hyphenation. Size: 12 points. Interline space: 15 points. Tracking: Normal. Line length: 21 picas.

Interline spacing is used to separate individual lines of type from each other. The visual space between lines should be greater than the interword space. Generous interline spacing ensures that the reader will be able to scan each line of the text without interruption.

Type style: Bodoni Bold. Alignment: Centered without hyphenation. Size: 12 points. Interline space: 16 points. Tracking: Normal. Line length: 24 picas.

Interline spacing is used to separate individual lines of type from each other. The visual space between lines should be greater than the interword space. Generous interline spacing ensures that the reader will be able to scan each line of the text without interruption.

Type style: Bodoni. Size: 18 points. Tracking: -5/200 em. Horizontal scale: 250%.

Bodoni

Type style: Bodoni Bold. Oblique: 13 degrees. Size: 18 points. Tracking: Normal.

Bodoni

Type style: Bodoni Bold. Size: 18 points. Horizontal scale: 80%.

Bodoni

Type style: Bodoni Bold. Size: 18 points. Tracking: -10/200 em. Horizontal scale: 250%.

Bodoni

Type style: Bodoni Poster. Oblique: 13 degrees. Size: 18 points. Tracking: Normal.

Bodoni

Type style: Bodoni Poster. Size: 18 points. Tracking: +5/200 em. Horizontal scale: 80%.

Bodoni

Type style: Bodoni Poster. Size: 18 points. Tracking: -5/200 em. Horizontal scale: 225%.

Characteristics

Bookman is a contemporary type fashioned after the traditional look of old style roman type. It is available on many different word processing and computer typesetting platforms. The light type style is used for text applications and the medium works well for headlines and subheads. The thin strokes of the characters are relatively heavy. The character widths of the letters are wide so

Bookman is good only in situations where you have wide columns. The bracketed serifs visually connect the letters and establish a comfortable horizontal eye movement. Some letters' serifs should actually overlap each other even with normal tracking. The ascenders and descenders are very short and stylistically look cramped because of the extremely high x-height. This means

that Bookman should have extra interline spacing to make reading more comfortable. Bookman is a great type for designing periodicals and booklets with a personal touch. It prints well on a variety of papers, uncoated and coated. Use Bookman for printed materials where the idea is contemporary and the mood is traditional.

Type styles:

Light

Light Italic

Medium

Medium Italic

Type style: Bookman Light. Size 48 points.

ABCDEFGHIJ
KLMNOPQRST
UVWXYZabcd
efghijklmnopqr
stuvwxyz1234

Tracking. Type style: Bookman Light. Size: 10 points.

Tracking adjusts interletter and interword spacing. Very tight (-3/200 em)

Tracking adjusts interletter and interword spacing. Tight -1/200 em)

Tracking adjusts interletter and interword spacing. Normal

Tracking adjusts interletter and interword spacing. Loose (+1/200 em)

Tracking adjusts interletter and interword spacing. Very loose (+3/200 em)

Tips

- Bookman text reproduces well using budget printing methods and inexpensive paper.
- Make heads and subheads with Bookman Medium horizontally scaled from 150 to 250 percent.
- Use a horizontal scale of 80 percent to produce condensed versions of Bookman Light and Medium.

- Bookman Light doesn't read well in sizes smaller than 10 points.
- Don't mix Bookman with other serif type styles such as Caslon or Bodoni.
- Try mixing Bookman with nongeometric sans serif typefaces, such as Helvetica Bold or Black, for headlines and subheads.
- For flush left alignment use 130 percent of the type size for interline spacing.

- With justified text you should use 140 percent of the type size for interline space.
- Normal tracking produces the most readable text. Try tight and very tight settings in stylistic situations.
- Gives a traditional look to business brochures, advertising and in-house reports.
- Mood reference: see Traditional, pages 46-55.

Type style: Bookman Light. Alignment: Flush left/ragged right. Size: 10 points. Interline space: 13 points. Tracking: Normal. Line Length: 19 picas.

Interline spacing is used to separate individual lines of type from each other. The visual space between lines should be greater than the interword space. Generous interline spacing ensures that the reader will be able to scan each line of the text without interruption.

Type style: Bookman Light. Alignment: Justified. Size: 10 points. Interline space: 14 points. Tracking: Normal. Line length: 19 picas.

Interline spacing is used to separate individual lines of type from each other. The visual space between lines should be greater than the interword space. Generous interline spacing ensures that the reader will be able to scan each line of the text without interruption.

Type style: Bookman Light. Alignment: Centered. Size: 10 points. Interline space: 15 points. Tracking: Normal. Line length: 22 picas.

Interline spacing is used to separate individual lines of type from each other. The visual space between lines should be greater than the interword space. Generous interline spacing ensures that the reader will be able to scan each line of the text without interruption.

Type style: Bookman Light. Size: 18 points. Tracking: Normal. Horizontal scale: 80%.

Bookman

Type style: Bookman Light. Size: 18 points. Tracking: -³⁄₂₀₀ em. Horizontal scale: 150%.

Bookman

Type style: Bookman Light Italic. Size: 18 points. Tracking: Normal. Horizontal scale: 80%.

Bookman

Type style: Bookman Medium. Size: 18 points. Tracking: Normal. Horizontal scale: 80%.

Bookman

Type style: Bookman Medium. Size: 18 points. Tracking: -³⁄₂₀₀ em. Horizontal scale: 150%.

Bookman

Type style: Bookman Medium. Size: 18 points. Tracking: -⁵⁄₂₀₀ em. Horizontal scale: 250%.

Bookman

Type style: Bookman Medium Italic. Size: 18 points. Tracking: -³⁄₂₀₀ em. Horizontal scale: 150%.

Bookman

Characteristics

This contemporary design originated as a signage alphabet. Later, additional variations were developed for print. Although it is missing condensed and expanded versions, it is very adaptable to optical and electronic modifications. This family of type styles was developed as a system of styles to provide a wide range of weights suitable for many applications. Each style was numbered instead of being assigned a name that might be misleading to the typographer. Frutiger's individual characters are carefully detailed and fitted for digital typesetting. The counters, or negative spaces, are uniquely shaped and are large enough to permit good legibility in small sizes or at a distance. The x-height is high but carefully proportioned to optimize the distinctive shapes of the ascenders and descenders without making them too short. The strokes are terminated horizontally and vertically but they are slightly angled, (see *S*, *G*, *c* and *g*). This adds a spirit to the letters that geometric regularity could not achieve. Frutiger is a playful type style with excellent legibility that will add warmth to the information you are presenting.

Type styles:

Frutiger 45

Frutiger 46

Frutiger 55

Frutiger 56

Frutiger 65

Frutiger 66

Frutiger 75

Frutiger 76

Frutiger 85

Type style: Frutiger 55. Size: 48 points.

ABCDEFGHIJKL
MNOPQRSTUV
WXYZabcdefghi
jklmnopqrstuvw
xyz12345&67890

Tracking. Type style: Frutiger 55. Size: 10 points

Tracking adjusts interletter and interword spacing. Very tight (-$\frac{9}{200}$ em)

Tracking adjusts interletter and interword spacing. Tight. (-$\frac{4}{200}$ em)

Tracking adjusts interletter and interword spacing. Normal

Tracking adjusts interletter and interword spacing. Loose (+$\frac{4}{200}$ em)

Tracking adjusts interletter and interword spacing. Very loose (+$\frac{9}{200}$ em)

Tips

- The letters lend themselves perfectly to oblique slanting and horizontal expansion of characters to 200 percent.
- Horizontal scaling works well between 80 or 90 percent; avoid lower percentages that produce distorted thin vertical strokes.
- Use normal letterspacing and 120 percent interline space.
- The wide selection of available weights and styles permits designing within the family.
- Frutiger 65 and 75 heads will work well with condensed gothics and old style roman text type styles.
- Avoid tight tracking because the distinctive letterforms are difficult to read.
- Use Frutiger in small text sizes with confidence that it will be legible.
- Frutiger works well flush left with tight or loose ragged right margins.
- Justified text situations require 140 percent of the type size for interline spacing.
- Use for advertising, corporate publications, signage and brochures.
- Mood reference: see Playful, pages 66-75.

Type style: Frutiger 55. Alignment: Flush left/ragged right. Size: 10 points. Interline space: 12 points. Tracking: Normal. Line length: 18 picas.

Interline spacing is used to separate individual lines of type from each other. The visual space between lines should be greater than the interword space. Generous interline spacing ensures that the reader will be able to scan each line of the text without interruption.

Type style: Frutiger 65. Alignment: Flush left/ragged right. Size: 10 points. Interline space: 13 points. Tracking: Normal. Line length: 18 picas.

Interline spacing is used to separate individual lines of type from each other. The visual space between lines should be greater than the interword space. Generous interline spacing ensures that the reader will be able to scan each line of the text without interruption.

Type style: Frutiger 55. Alignment: Justified. Size: 10 points. Interline space: 16 points. Tracking: Normal. Line length: 18 picas.

Interline spacing is used to separate individual lines of type from each other. The visual spacing between lines should always be greater than the interword space. Generous interline spacing ensures that the reader will be able to scan each line of the text without interruption.

Type style: Frutiger 65. Size: 18 points. Tracking: + 1/200 em. Horizontal scale: 80%.

Frutiger

Type style: Frutiger 85. Size: 18 points. Tracking: + 1/200 em. Horizontal scale: 80%.

Frutiger

Type style: Frutiger 55. Size: 18 points. Tracking: - 2/200 em. Horizontal scale: 125%.

Frutiger

Type style: Frutiger 65. Size: 18 points. Tracking: - 3/200 em. Horizontal scale: 150%.

Type style: Frutiger 75. Size: 18 points. Tracking: - 5/200 em. Horizontal scale: 150%.

Type style: Frutiger 85. Size: 18 points. Tracking: - 6/200 em. Horizontal scale: 200%.

Type style: Frutiger 85. Size: 18 points. Tracking: Normal. Oblique: 13 degrees.

Frutiger

Characteristics

The condensed type styles of the Helvetica family are not as well known as the regular Helvetica roman. This family is representative of the sans serif types based on nineteenth-century faces like News Gothic and Franklin Gothic. Using Helvetica Condensed increases the character count without sacrificing legibility. The characters are formed with a high x-height. The ascenders and descenders are short but not cramped and their distinct shapes make it easy to read. Since the ascenders and descenders are short, it is necessary to use ample interline space. The lowercase letter styles provide good horizontal eye movement when used in short line measures. The lowercase letter *a* is designed in the tradition of the old style roman *a*. This style of *a* is easier to read than *a*'s that are shaped like the *c, e* and *o*. As an example compare the Helvetica *a* with the Avant Garde *a* on page 4. The elegant shapes of the compressed letters give an aggressive straightforward look to a message.

Type styles:

Light

Light Oblique

Condensed

Oblique

Bold

Bold Oblique

Black

Black Oblique

Compressed

Extra Compressed

Ultra Compressed

Type style: Helvetica Condensed Bold. Size: 48 points.

ABCDEFGHIJKLMN OPQRSTUVWXYZa bcdefghijklmnopqr stuvwxyz12345&6 7890!$?()%¢£"".:,,

Tracking. Type style: Helvetica Condensed Bold. Size:12 points.

Tracking adjusts interletter and interword spacing. Very tight (-3/200 em)

Tracking adjusts interletter and interword spacing. Tight (-1/200 em)

Tracking adjusts interletter and interword spacing. Normal

Tracking adjusts interletter and interword spacing. Loose (+1/200 em)

Tracking adjusts interletter and interword spacing. Very loose (+3/200 em)

Tips

- Helvetica Condensed and Compressed should be tracked normally. Legibility is impaired with tight settings.
- Helvetica Condensed sets well in very small sizes and works well as text.
- The Bold, Black Condensed and Compressed versions mix well with regular proportioned Helvetica and other regular gothics, but not with other condensed styles or geometric gothics.
- Condensed Black and Compressed are ideal styles for horizontal scaling up to 400 percent.
- All versions can be horizontally scaled to 80 percent if necessary.
- Text sets best with a flush left alignment. With justified alignment, additional interline space is necessary to compensate for wider than normal interword spaces.
- Form oblique versions of the Compressed styles by slanting the letters 13 degrees.
- Helvetica Condensed and Compressed are perfect for text and headlines on industrial brochures, logos and exhibit graphics.
- Mood reference: see Aggressive, pages 76-85.

Type style: Helvetica Condensed Bold. Alignment: Flush left/ragged right. Size: 12 points. Interline space: 15 points. Tracking: Normal. Line length: 21 picas.

Interline spacing is used to separate individual lines of type from each other. The visual space between lines should be greater than the interword space. Generous interline spacing ensures that the reader will be able to scan each line of the text without interruption.

Type style: Helvetica Condensed Black. Alignment: Flush left/ragged right. Size: 12 points. Interline space: 16 points. Tracking: Normal. Line length: 20 picas.

Interline spacing is used to separate individual lines of type from each other. The visual space between lines should be greater than the interword space. Generous interline spacing ensures that the reader will be able to scan each line of the text without interruption.

Type style: Helvetica Condensed Bold. Alignment: Justified. Size: 12 points. Interline space: 17 points. Tracking: Normal. Line length: 20 picas.

Interline spacing is used to separate individual lines of type from each other. The visual space between lines should be greater than the interword space. Generous interline spacing ensures that the reader will be able to scan each line of the text without interruption.

Type style: Helvetica Condensed Bold. Size: 18 points. Tracking: Normal. Horizontal scale: 80%.

Helvetica

Type style: Helvetica Condensed Black. Size: 18 points. Tracking: -1/200 em. Horizontal scale: 80%.

Helvetica

Type style: Helvetica Compressed. Size: 18 points. Tracking: +3/200 em. Horizontal scale: 80%.

Helvetica

Type style: Helvetica Condensed Black. Size: 18 points. Tracking: Normal. Oblique: 13 degrees.

Helvetica

Type style: Helvetica Extra Compressed. Size: 18 points. Tracking: Normal. Oblique: 13 degrees.

Helvetica

Type style: Helvetica Extra Compressed. Size: 18 points. Tracking: -3/200 em. Horizontal scale: 400%.

Type style: Helvetica Compressed. Size: 18 points. Tracking: Normal. Horizontal scale: 200%. Oblique: 13 degrees.

Characteristics

Optima is considered a sans serif typeface although its character is drawn from the classic roman letter. Consider Optima an elegant serif-less roman with the straightforwardness of a gothic sans serif. Optima replaces the serif at the end of each stroke with a flair and a cupped terminal. The capitals are wide and full bodied as in classic roman design. The O and other letters are actually wider than the cap height. This opens the counter space of the letters and necessitates using normal to loose letterspacing. The lowercase letters display a calligraphic thin-to-thick relationship unlike sans serifs type styles. The old style roman lower case g is used to distinguish the difference between it and the modern q letterform. Optima's x-height is high, but it also features relatively long ascenders and descenders. While this is a contradiction in terms, the italics are actually oblique letterforms. This is a one-of-a-kind design that brings a friendly presence to any printed piece.

Type styles:

Optima

Italic

Bold

Bold Italic

Type style: Optima. Size: 48 points.

ABCDEFGHIJKLM
NOPQRSTUVWX
YZabcdefghijklmn
opqrstuvwxyz123
45&67890!$?()%"

Tracking. Type style: Optima. Size: 12 points.

Tracking adjusts interletter and interword spacing. Very tight (-$\frac{5}{200}$ em)

Tracking adjusts interletter and interword spacing. Tight (-$\frac{1}{200}$ em)

Tracking adjusts interletter and interword spacing. Normal

Tracking adjusts interletter and interword spacing. Loose (+$\frac{1}{200}$ em)

Tracking adjusts interletter and interword spacing. Very loose (+$\frac{5}{200}$ em)

Tips

- Although Optima comes in a limited variety of weights you can use it exclusively.
- You can also mix Optima with almost any other type style, but avoid using other sans serifs that have a calligraphic flair; they will produce a visual conflict between faces.
- Use text sizes 12 points and larger; Optima's subtleties are just not apparent in the small sizes.
- Optima is not a good choice for large amounts of text because it lacks the serifs of a roman that provide a horizontal flow.
- Avoid setting Optima justified because the variable interword and interletter space produces an irregular text color.
- This face enjoys openness between letters as well as between lines.
- Electronic horizontal expansion of Optima Bold works very well for headlines.
- Avoid horizontal scaling below 90 percent. The tight versions simply deny the character of the type style.
- Use Optima for community service brochures, announcements, advertising and corporate promotional literature.
- Mood reference: see Friendly, pages 86-95.

Type style: Optima. Alignment: Flush left/ragged right. Size: 12 points. Interline space: 15 points. Tracking: Normal. Line length: 24 picas.

Interline spacing is used to separate individual lines of type from each other. The visual space between lines should be greater than the interword space. Generous interline spacing ensures that the reader will be able to scan each line of the text without interruption.

Type style: Optima Bold. Alignment: Flush left/ragged right. Size: 12 points. Interline space: 16 points. Tracking: Normal. Line length: 24 picas.

Interline spacing is used to separate individual lines of type from each other. The visual space between lines should be greater than the interword space. Generous interline spacing ensures that the reader will be able to scan each line of the text without interruption.

Type style: Optima. Alignment: Centered. Size: 14 points. Interline space: 18 points. Tracking: Normal. Line length: 24 picas.

Interline spacing is used to separate individual lines of type from each other. The visual space between lines should be greater than the interword space. Generous interline spacing ensures that the reader will be able to scan each line of the text without interruption.

Type style: Optima. Size: 18 points. Tracking: Normal. Horizontal scale: 90%.

Optima

Type style: Optima Italic. Size: 18 points. Tracking: Normal. Horizontal scale: 90%.

Optima

Type style: Optima. Size: 18 points. Tracking: -5/200 em. Horizontal scale: 150%.

Optima

Type style: Optima Bold. Size: 18 points. Tracking: -8/200 em. Horizontal scale: 250%.

Type style: Optima Bold. Size: 18 points. Tracking: -1/200 em. Horizontal scale: 150%.

Type style: Optima Bold Italic. Size: 18 points. Tracking: -5/200 em. Horizontal scale: 150%.

Optima

Type style: Optima Bold. Size: 18 points. Tracking: -5/200 em. Horizontal scale: 200%.

Character

Syntax is a sans serif type style with classic proportioned roman capitals and gothic styled lowercase letters. Although the type style appears to have strokes of equal thickness, if you compare the strokes there is actually a significant difference in widths. Also, there are no straight lines. This type style is drawn using irregular line weights that make simple letters like the *f* and *t* distinctive. Letters like the *W* have strokes that terminate at right angles to the stroke rather than horizontal to the baseline. This styling of the terminals creates similarity between the capitals and lowercase letters. The high x-height makes the Syntax family easy to read even when set in small sizes. The lowercase letters produce a consistent text color and high degree of legibility even when set in a wide range of tracking styles. The gothic styled lowercase letters like the *a* and the *g* help make this type style very readable. Compare with the *a* and *g* in Avant Garde and Helvetica Condensed on pages 4 and 14. Syntax has a distinctive flair that combines the best of classic proportions and contemporary sans serif types.

Type styles:

Syntax

Italic

Bold

Black

Ultra Black

Type style: Syntax. Size: 48 points.

ABCDEFGHIJKLM
NOPQRSTUVWX
YZabcdefghijklmn
opqrstuvwxyz123
45&67890!$?()%

Tracking. Type style: Syntax. Size: 10 points.

Tracking adjusts interletter and interword spacing. Very tight (-$^3/_{200}$ em)

Tracking adjusts interletter and interword spacing. Tight (-$^1/_{200}$ em)

Tracking adjusts interletter and interword spacing. Normal

Tracking adjusts interletter and interword spacing. Loose (+$^1/_{200}$ em)

Tracking adjusts interletter and interword spacing. Very loose (+$^3/_{200}$ em)

Tips

- Text styles can be set as small as 8 points.
- The Syntax family prints well on both coated and uncoated paper stocks.
- You can set Syntax loose or tight, but it works best with normal tracking.
- Don't mix Syntax with other serif and sans serif families. Since there is a good range of styles represented in the family this isn't a problem.

- Slanted oblique versions of Bold, Black and Ultra Black created electronically or optically are compatible.
- Condensed versions of Syntax look stressed but you can horizontally scale the type styles to 80 percent.
- Black and Ultra Black type styles can be horizontally expanded up to 250 percent.
- Use 130 to 150 percent of type size for

interline spacing. The irregular mean line formed by the angular termination of the strokes requires extra interline space.
- Bold and Black type styles can be slanted to produce excellent oblique versions.
- Use Syntax to add a flair to any situation where a sans serif is called for.
- Mood reference: see Flair, pages 96-105.

Type style: Syntax. Alignment: Flush left/ragged right. Size: 10 points. Interline space: 13 points. Tracking: Normal. Line length: 20 picas.

Interline spacing is used to separate individual lines of type from each other. The visual space between lines should be greater than the interword space. Generous interline spacing ensures that the reader will be able to scan each line of the text without interruption.

Type style: Syntax Bold. Alignment: Flush left/ragged right. Size: 10 points. Interline space: 14 points. Tracking: Normal. Line length: 20 picas.

Interline spacing is used to separate individual lines of type from each other. The visual space between lines should be greater than the interword space. Generous interline spacing ensures that the reader will be able to scan each line of the text without interruption.

Type style: Syntax. Alignment: Justified. Size: 10 points. Interline space: 15 points. Tracking: Normal. Line length: 20 picas.

Interline spacing is used to separate individual lines of type from each other. The visual space between lines should be greater than the interword space. Generous interline spacing ensures that the reader will be able to scan each line of the text without interruption.

Type style: Syntax. Size: 18 points. Tracking: Normal. Horizontal scale: 80%.

Syntax

Type style: Syntax Black. Size: 18 points. Tracking: Normal. Horizontal scale: 80%.

Syntax

Type style: Syntax Black. Size: 18 points. Tracking: -⁵⁄₁₀₀ em. Horizontal scale: 250%.

Type style: Syntax Bold. Size: 18 points. Tracking: Normal. Oblique: 13 degrees.

Type style: Syntax Black. Size: 18 points. Tracking: Normal. Oblique: 13 degrees.

Type style: Syntax Ultra Black. Size: 18 points. Tracking: Normal. Oblique: 13 degrees.

Syntax

Type style: Syntax Ultra Black. Size: 18 points. Tracking: Normal. Oblique: 13 degrees. Horizontal scale: 250%.

Times Roman

Characteristics

Times Roman is a modern design based on traditional Dutch Old Style characteristics. It was designed as a newspaper type style with an emphasis on the craft and aesthetics required to produce the *London Times*. The heavier than normal thin strokes were designed to accommodate the coarse newsprint paper and long run press requirements. Times is a popular type style because of its readability and application to a wide range of print media. The letters are slightly condensed to increase the character count. Times Roman has a high x-height and distinctive counter forms that are easy to recognize. The lowercase characters are drawn with an oblique axis to establish a low weighted character. Letters such as the *a, c, d* and *e* show the low weighted stroke that emphasizes horizontal eye movement. Large bracketed serifs are used to link the characters. This horizontal connection is particularly important in a type style designed for short measures and justified alignment. Times Roman is a popular type style available on almost every word processor and typesetting system.

Type styles:

Times Roman

Italic

Bold

Bold Italic

Type style: Times Roman. Size: 48 points.

ABCDEFGHIJK
LMNOPQRSTU
VWXYZabcdefg
hijklmnopqrstuvw
xyz12345&67890

Tracking. Type style: Times Roman. Size: 11 points.

Tracking adjusts interletter and interword spacing. Very tight (-⁹⁄₂₀₀ em)

Tracking adjusts interletter and interword spacing. Tight (-⁵⁄₂₀₀ em)

Tracking adjusts interletter and interword spacing. Normal

Tracking adjusts interletter and interword spacing. Loose (+⁵⁄₂₀₀ em)

Tracking adjusts interletter and interword spacing. Very loose (+⁹⁄₂₀₀ em)

Tips

- Times works well in a wide range of sizes from 8 points.
- The type style prints well on both coated and uncoated papers.
- Times does not have a book weight so it prints darker than most romans.
- Works well for setting justified text.
- Avoid tight tracking. Times Roman was designed to accommodate loose interletter space but it does not like tight spacing.
- Normal interline space should be 120 percent of type size for left alignment and 130 percent of type size for justified text.
- Use horizontal scaling of 90 percent or less to create a workable condensed style.
- Expanded versions should be limited to display and headline applications.
- Times Roman Bold and Bold Italic can be horizontally scaled to 200 percent.
- Times Roman mixes well with almost all typefaces. Try using it with headlines set in a sans serif like Helvetica Bold or Black.
- Use Times Roman with the confidence that its informative character will function in almost any application.
- Mood reference: see Informative, pages 106-115.

Type style: Times Roman. Alignment: Flush left/ragged right. Size: 11 points. Interline space: 13 points. Tracking: Normal. Line length: 18 picas.

Interline spacing is used to separate individual lines of type from each other. The visual space between lines should be greater than the interword space. Generous interline spacing ensures that the reader will be able to scan each line of the text without interruption.

Type style: Times Roman Bold. Alignment: Flush left/ragged right. Size: 11 points. Interline space: 14 points. Tracking: Normal. Line length: 18 picas.

Interline spacing is used to separate individual lines of type from each other. The visual space between lines should be greater than the interword space. Generous interline spacing ensures that the reader will be able to scan each line of the text without interruption.

Type style: Times Roman. Alignment: Justified. Size: 11 points. Interline space: 14 points. Tracking: Normal. Line length: 18 picas.

Interline spacing is used to separate individual lines of type from each other. The visual space between lines should be greater than the interword space. Generous interline spacing ensures that the reader will be able to scan each line of the text without interruption.

Type style: Times Roman. Size: 18 points. Tracking: Normal. Horizontal scale: 90%.

Times

Type style: Times Roman. Size: 18 points. Tracking: -1/200 em. Horizontal scale: 120%.

Times

Type style: Times Roman. Size: 18 points. Tracking: -5/200 em. Horizontal scale: 200%.

Times

Type style: Times Roman Bold. Size: 18 points. Tracking: Normal. Horizontal scale: 90%.

Times

Type style: Times Roman Bold. Size: 18 points. Tracking: Normal. Horizontal scale: 120%.

Times

Type style: Times Roman Bold. Size: 18 points. Tracking: -5/200 em. Horizontal scale: 200%.

Times

Type style: Times Roman Bold Italic. Size: 18 points. Tracking: -5/200 em. Horizontal scale: 200%.

Times

Characteristics

Trump is a roman type style that strongly reflects a calligraphic style. Individual letters are carefully drawn with pen and brush detailing to create a distinct set of characters. The counter shapes are beautifully crafted and distinctively formed so that any similarity that two characters might have is minimized. Look for the old style back-slanted vertical axis in the round letters like the capital *O* and lower case *e*. The strokes are terminated with strong serifs that visually connect the letters of a word. Look at lowercase letters like the *a*, *b*, *n* and *r* for the distinctive calligraphic angles that contribute to Trump's easy reading. Trump has a medium x-height and medium length ascenders and descenders. The length of the ascenders contributes to the easy eye movement across the mean line. Trump reads very well with normal tracking but it also tolerates the variable interletter and interword space when set with justified alignment. The formal beauty and the fine attention to mechanical details projects a look of sophistication on the printed page.

Type styles:

Trump

Italic

Bold

Bold Italic

Type style: Trump. Size: 48 points.

ABCDEFGHIJK
LMNOPQRST
UVWXYZabcde
fghijklmnopqrst
uvwxyz12345&

Tracking. Type style: Trump. Size: 11 points.

Tracking adjusts interletter and interword spacing. Very tight (-⁹⁄₂₀₀ em)

Tracking adjusts interletter and interword spacing. Tight (-⁴⁄₂₀₀ em)

Tracking adjusts interletter and interword spacing. Normal

Tracking adjusts interletter and interword spacing. Loose (+⁵⁄₂₀₀ em)

Tracking adjusts interletter and interword spacing. Very loose (+⁹⁄₂₀₀ em)

Tips

- Set Trump in sizes 11 points and larger to take advantage of the type styles' character.
- Trump works well with justified alignment.
- Use line lengths of 20 picas or longer.
- This type style is well suited to setting text with centered alignment.
- Do not mix Trump with other romans.
- Trump text can be mixed with bold and extra bold sans serif type such as Helvetica.

- Use horizontal scaling of 90 percent for condensed text applications.
- Try using Trump Bold with horizontal scaling of 200 percent for heads and subheads.
- Avoid tight tracking but don't worry if a few serifs overprint each other.
- Headlines or subheads set in all capitals should be loosely tracked and carefully letter spaced for visual uniformity.

- Trump prints well on uncoated papers.
- Minimum interline spacing should be 130 percent of the type size.
- Use Trump in fine books, specialty brochures, display type and any application that needs a touch of sophistication.
- Mood reference: see Sophistication, pages 116-125.

Type style: Trump. Alignment: Flush left/ragged right. Size: 11 points. Interline space: 14 points. Tracking: Normal. Line length: 20 picas.

Interline spacing is used to separate individual lines of type from each other. The visual space between lines should be greater than the interword space. Generous interline spacing ensures that the reader will be able to scan each line of the text without interruption.

Type style: Trump Bold. Alignment: Centered. Size: 11 points. Interline space: 15 points. Tracking: Normal. Line length: 20 picas.

Interline spacing is used to separate individual lines of type from each other. The visual space between lines should be greater than the interword space. Generous interline spacing ensures that the reader will be able to scan each line of the text without interruption.

Type style: Trump. Alignment: Justified. Size: 11 points. Interline space: 15 points. Tracking: Normal. Line length: 20 picas.

Interline spacing is used to separate individual lines of type from each other. The visual space between lines should be greater than the interword space. Generous interline spacing ensures that the reader will be able to scan each line of the text without interruption.

Type style: Trump. Size: 18 points. Tracking: Normal. Horizontal scale: 90%.

Trump

Type style: Trump. Size: 18 points. Tracking: Normal. Horizontal scale: 150%.

Trump

Type style: Trump. Size: 18 points. Tracking: Normal. Horizontal scale: 200%.

Trump

Type style: Trump Bold. Size: 18 points. Tracking: Normal. Horizontal scale: 90%.

Trump

Type style: Trump Bold. Size: 18 points. Tracking: Normal. Horizontal scale: 150%.

Trump

Type style: Trump Bold. Size: 18 points. Tracking: -³⁄₂₀₀ em. Horizontal scale: 200%.

Type style: Trump Bold Italic. Size: 18 points. Tracking: -³⁄₂₀₀ em. Horizontal scale: 200%.

Part 2:
Type Moods and
Design Options

About Type Moods

This section provides a collection of type effects recipes that can be used for many design situations. Here you'll find applications that lend themselves to direct or modified use in the work you do for your clients.

What Are Moods?

Type mood refers to the meaning or feeling associated with a type style. The particular mood projected by a type style is in part the result of social and technological conditions that affected the original design. Mood is also dependent on the individual reader or viewer and their personal taste and previous experience. Using a particular type style cannot change the meaning of the words, but it can enhance the message.

How to Use this Section.

The moods presented in this section correspond with the type styles in Section 1. Five different businesses are used to illustrate each mood. The sample businesses represent typical clients of a small studio or a freelance designer. A variety of business profiles shows that each type style can be used for a variety of companies. For example, Caslon has been used to project a classic image for a string quartet, bookshop, clothing store, wedding consultant, and an attorney. Since each business is represented in more than one mood category, you will be able to see how the same company's image is changed by simply substituting type styles.

If your needs are to lift'n'match ideas for your clients' applications or simply to gather ideas, you will develop a clearer understanding of type moods after studying this section. The examples should serve as a resource for generating your own ideas; and possibly you'll find a few ready-made solutions.

Trendy

Trendy represents a popular look of the times. Although this is a style that changes, some things don't seem to change quickly. Avant Garde will create ads and displays that appear to be on the leading edge of fashion. It's simple to use; the geometric styling looks new and refreshing however it is applied.

Nostalgic

Type that is nostalgic makes us think of the late nineteenth and early twentieth centuries. You can use Bodoni to create the exciting eclectic designs that reflect the letterform styles of the period. Bodoni comes in many different drawings and weights, and it is easily modified to create many additional type styles.

24

Traditional

The reader is comfortable when the mood is traditional. Readers or viewers see what they expect to see in the presentation of the material. A traditional mood is easily established using a type style like Bookman. It was designed as a modern type style that would be acceptable in all situations and for all audiences.

Classic

A classic mood brings a quiet natural balance to typographic composition. I used Caslon to represent it. A classic mood should include symmetrical composition and large point sizes. If you want to bring the true elegance of the hand-drawn Roman letter to today's printed communications, try Caslon.

Playful

A playful mood is entertaining and lighthearted. I selected Frutiger to illustrate playful because its characters are based on the unique contrasts of curved and straight shapes. A playful composition incorporates contrasts, and will most often have an intuitive appearance.

Aggressive

An aggressive mood creates a strong imperative that demands a response from the viewer. There is a sense of importance and truth implied in the use of a type style like Helvetica Condensed, and particularly the Compressed and Extra Compressed versions.

Friendly

This mood is comfortable. it's easy to read and personally appealing. I selected Optima because it combines the best characteristics of both sans serif and serif designs. Optima will create a warm personal presence, whether you use all capitals, obliques or lowercase combinations.

Flair

If a type style has flair, it has a special character that makes it unique. Many contemporary type styles have been designed for their novelty, but to have flair, a character must also have a sense of style and fashion. The strokes of Syntax are terminated at irregular oblique angles, a distinction that gives this sans serif type style a notable flair.

Informative

An informative mood suggests that the transfer of information is the primary concern. This requires a straightforward presentation of the reading material through the composition of the page elements. Most type styles are informative as opposed to decorative, and there is no condition that limits informative type styles to only serif styles. However, for this book I chose Times Roman to illustrate the informative mood.

Sophisticated

A sophisticated mood implies a sense of something fine or beautiful. The symbolic characteristics that are associated with being sophisticated include a visual refinement of the letterforms and careful attention to conventional values in composition. Trump works well for applications requiring a sophisticated mood.

Make Your Own Moods.

As you work with type styles to create new moods, the unique characteristics of type that produce a mood will become obvious to you. Using what I have introduced you to in this section as a foundation, you can create many new recipes of your own.

The Body Shop logos demonstrate how Avant Garde can be stretched and electronically modified to suggest a contemporary styled fitness center.

Logos

1. ***The/Shop.*** Type style: Avant Garde Demi.
   BODY. Type style: Avant Garde Demi. Kerning: Very tight.
2. ***The Body Shop.*** Type style: Avant Garde Demi.
3. ***The/Shop.*** Type style: Avant Garde Demi.
   BODY. Type style: Avant Garde Demi. Scale: Free form.
4. ***The Body Shop.*** Type style: Avant Garde Demi. Baseline: Free form curve.
5. ***The/Shop.*** Type style: Avant Garde Demi.
   BODY. Type style: Avant Garde Demi. Horizontal scale: 50%.

Applications

Logo. ***The/Shop.*** Type style: Avant Garde Demi. ***BODY.*** Type style: Avant Garde Demi outlined.

6. **Envelope.** ***Logo.*** (#10 business)
   Address/Title. Type style: Avant Garde Book. Size: 10 points. Interline: 12 points.
7. **Business Card.** (3.5x2) ***Logo.***
   Tag line. Type style: Avant Garde Demi. Size: 18 points.
   Address. Type style: Avant Garde Book. Size: 10 points. Interline: 12 points.
   Name/Phone. Type style: Avant Garde Demi. Size: 11 points.
8. **T-Shirt.** ***Logo.***

The BODY Shop

1

The Body Shop

2

THE BODY SHOP

3

The Body Shop

4

the BODY shop

5

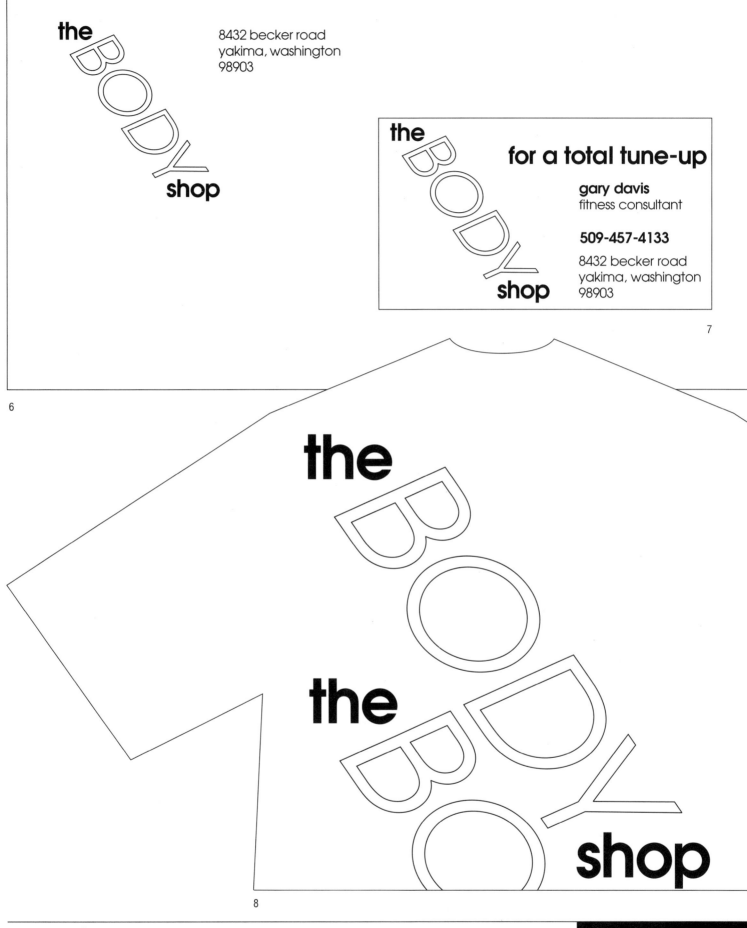

the **BODY** shop

8432 becker road
yakima, washington
98903

the **BODY** shop

for a total tune-up

gary davis
fitness consultant

509-457-4133

8432 becker road
yakima, washington
98903

7

6

the **BODY** shop

the **BODY** shop

8

The Tigger Too logos show how the geometric simplicity of Avant Garde can be used as a decorative device and for creating patterns in the applications.

Logos

1. **TIGGER T**. Type style: Avant Garde Demi. Horizontal scale: 80%.
   OO. Type style: Avant Garde Book. Horizontal scale: 300%.
2. **TT.** Type style: Avant Garde Demi Oblique. Horizontal scale: 250%.
   TIGGER/TOO. Type style: Avant Garde Demi. Horizontal scale: 70%.
3. **TIGGER TOO**. Type style: Avant Garde Demi. Horizontal scale: 150%.
4. **TIGGER TOO**. Type style: Avant Garde Demi. Scale: Free form.
5. **TT.** Type style: Avant Garde Book. Scale: Free form.
   Tigger/Too. Type style: Avant Garde Book Oblique.

Applications

   Logo. TT. Type style: Avant Garde Demi. Proportional scale: 200%.
   Tigger/Too. Type style: Avant Garde Demi.
6. **Business Card.** (3.5x2) **Logo.**
   Tag line. Type style: Avant Garde Demi. Size: 11 points.
   Name/Phone. Type style: Avant Garde Demi. Size: 8 points.
   Address/Title. Type style: Avant Garde Book. Size: 8 points. Interline: 10 points.
7. **Letterhead.** (8.5x11) **Logo.**
   Tag line. Type style: Avant Garde Demi. Size: 11 points. Interline: 13 points.
   Address/Phone. Type style: Avant Garde Book. Size: 8 points. Interline: 10 points.
8. **Newspaper Ad.** (2.5x6.25) **Logo.**
   Features/Phone. Type style: Avant Garde Demi. Size: 12 points. Interline: 15 points.
   Address/Services. Type style: Avant Garde Book. Size: 10 points. Interline: 12 points.

1

2

3

4

5

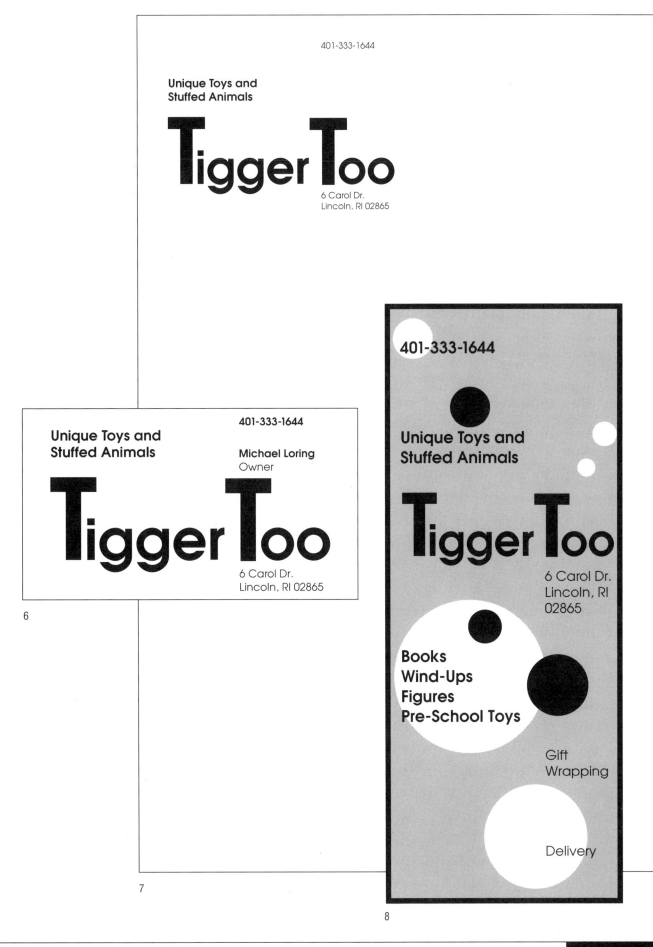

401-333-1644

Unique Toys and
Stuffed Animals

Tigger Too

6 Carol Dr.
Lincoln, RI 02865

Unique Toys and
Stuffed Animals

401-333-1644

Michael Loring
Owner

Tigger Too

6 Carol Dr.
Lincoln, RI 02865

6

7

401-333-1644

Unique Toys and
Stuffed Animals

Tigger Too

6 Carol Dr.
Lincoln, RI
02865

Books
Wind-Ups
Figures
Pre-School Toys

Gift
Wrapping

Delivery

8

The new and fresh look of Avant Garde produces a contemporary image for the Odilon apparel shop.

Logos

1. *Odilon.* Type style: Avant Garde Book Oblique. Horizontal scale: 300%. Effect: Overprint.
2. *Odilon.* Type style: Avant Garde Demi with back-slant shadow. Horizontal scale: 200%.
3. *Odilon.* Type style: Avant Garde Book Oblique. Horizontal scale: 250%.
4. *Odilon.* Type style: Avant Garde Demi outlined. Horizontal scale: 250%.
5. *ODILON.* Type style: Avant Garde Demi. Baseline: Circular.

Applications

Logo. Type style: Avant Garde Demi Oblique. *O.* Type style: Avant Garde Demi.

6. **Business Card.** (3.5x2) *Logo. Name/Tag line/Phone.* Type style: Avant Garde Demi. Size: 9 points. Interline space: 10 points. *Title/Address.* Type style: Avant Garde Book. Size: 8 points. Interline space: 11 points.
7. **Price Tag.** (2x4.25) *Logo. Style/Code.* Type style: Avant Garde Book. Size: 10 points. *Size/Price.* Type style: Avant Garde Demi. Size: 14 points
8. **Shopping Bag.** *Logo.*

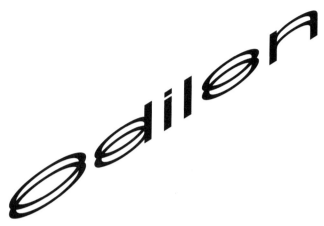

1

2

3

4

5

Monica Loring
Owner

ODILON
Contemporary Apparel, Fashion Footwear, Accessories

1927 Bridge Street
Nashua, NH 03061
803-882-5242

6

ODILON

STYLE #
CODE #

SIZE

PRICE

7

8

Avant Garde

Even though DeVors & Co. sells old and used books, Avant Garde was used to suggest a very modern and efficient business.

Logos

1. ***DeVors/Co.*** Type style: Avant Garde Demi.
   &. Type style: Avant Garde Book.
2. ***DeVors & Co.*** Type style: Avant Garde Demi Oblique. Horizontal scale: 80%.
3. ***DeVors & Co.*** Type style: Avant Garde Demi. Horizontal scale: 150%.
4. ***DeVors & Co.*** Type style: Avant Garde Book. Horizontal scale: 60%.
5. ***DeVors/Co.*** Type style: Avant Garde Demi Oblique.
   &. Type style: Avant Garde Book.

Applications

   Logo. ***DeVors/Co.*** Type style: Avant Garde Book. ***&.*** Type style: Avant Garde Demi.
6. **Letterhead.** (8.5x11) ***Logo.***
   Tag line. Type style: Avant Garde Demi. Size: 10 points. Interline: 12 points.
   Address. Type style: Avant Garde Book. Size: 8 points. Interline: 10 points.
7. **Business Card.** (2x3.5) ***Logo.***
   Tag line/Name/Title. Type style: Avant Garde Demi. Size: 10 points. Interline: 12 points.
   Address. Type style: Avant Garde Book. Size: 8 points. Interline: 10 points.
8. **Newspaper Ad** (2.5x6.25) ***Logo.***
   Tag line/Phone. Type style: Avant Garde Demi. Size: 14 points. Interline: 16 points.
   Address. Type style: Avant Garde Book. Size: 11 points. Interline: 13 points.

1

2

3

4

5

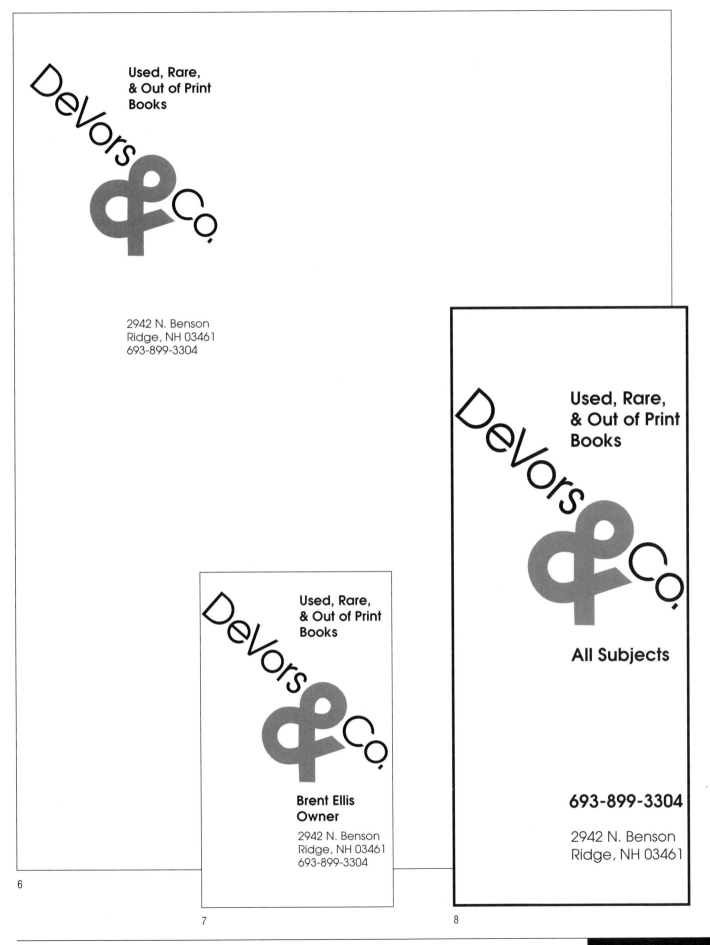

**Used, Rare,
& Out of Print
Books**

2942 N. Benson
Ridge, NH 03461
693-899-3304

**Used, Rare,
& Out of Print
Books**

**Brent Ellis
Owner**

2942 N. Benson
Ridge, NH 03461
693-899-3304

**Used, Rare,
& Out of Print
Books**

All Subjects

693-899-3304

2942 N. Benson
Ridge, NH 03461

6

7

8

Bodoni gives Anson C. Borst and Associates a professional image of practicing law the old-fashioned way.

Logos

1. *A.* Type style: Bodoni Poster. Horizontal scale: 85%.
   Anson C. Borst and Associates. Type style: Bodoni Bold Condensed.
2. *A.* Type style: Bodoni Poster. Horizontal scale: 85%.
   Anson C. Borst/Associates. Type style: Bodoni Black. Horizontal scale: 85%.
   and. Type style: Bodoni Bold Condensed.
3. *AAA.* Type style: Bodoni Black. Horizontal scale: 85%.
   Anson C. Borst and Associates. Type style: Bodoni Bold Condensed.
4. *a*. Type style: Bodoni Black Italic. Horizontal scale: 85%.
   anson c. borst and associates. Type style: Bodoni Italic. Horizontal scale: 85%.
5. *Anson C. Borst and Associates.* Type style: Bodoni Bold Condensed.

Applications

Logo. *Anson C. Borst/Associates.* Type style: Bodoni Bold Condensed. *and.* Type style: Bodoni Bold Italic.

6. **Invoice.** (8.5x11) *Logo.*
   Tag line/Invoice. Type style: Bodoni Black Italic. Size: 12 points.
   Name/Phone/Address/Information. Type style: Bodoni Black Italic. Size: 9 points. Interline: 12 points.
7. **Envelope.** (#10 business) *Logo.*
   Tag line. Type style: Bodoni Black Italic. Size: 12 points.
   Address. Type style: Bodoni Black Italic. Size: 8 points. Interline: 11 points.
8. **Business Card.** (3.5x2) *Logo.*
   Tag line. Type style: Bodoni Black Italic. Size: 12 points.
   Name/Address. Type style: Bodoni Black Italic. Size: 8 points. Interline: 11 points.

1

2

3

4

Anson C. Borst and Associates

5

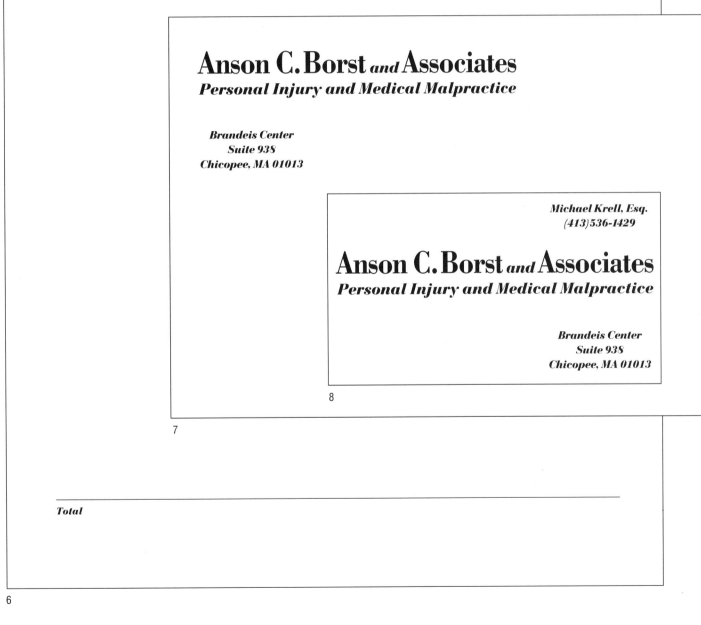

Michael Krell, Esq.
(413)536-1429

Anson C. Borst *and* Associates
Personal Injury and Medical Malpractice

Brandeis Center
Suite 938
Chicopee, MA 01013

Invoice

Date:
Client Number:
Matter Number:

Anson C. Borst *and* Associates
Personal Injury and Medical Malpractice

Brandeis Center
Suite 938
Chicopee, MA 01013

Michael Krell, Esq.
(413)536-1429

Anson C. Borst *and* Associates
Personal Injury and Medical Malpractice

Brandeis Center
Suite 938
Chicopee, MA 01013

8

7

Total

6

Bodoni's romantic design characteristics are perfect for creating a lively image for Scaletti's Italian Restaurant.

Logos

1. *scaletti's.* Type style: Bodoni Black.
2. *Scaletti's.* Type style: Bodoni Poster outlined.
3. *Scaletti's.* Type style: Bodoni Black Italic.
4. *S*. Type style: Bodoni Black Italic. .
   Scaletti's. Type style: Bodoni Poster.
5. *S*. Type style: Bodoni Bold. Horizontal scale: 200%.
   scaletti's. Type style: Bodoni Poster. Horizontal scale: 85%.

Applications

   Logo. *SCALETTI'S.* Type style: Bodoni Bold.
6. **Menu.** (5.5x17) *Logo.*
   Date. Type style: Bodoni Bold. Size: 40 points.
7. **Newspaper Ad.** (2.5x3) *Logo.*
   Features. Type style: Bodoni Black. Size: 10 points. Interline: 11 points.
   Phone. Type style: Bodoni Black. Size: 15 points.
   Address. Type style: Bodoni Black. Size: 8 points. Interline: 10 points.
8. **Order Form.** (5x7) *Logo.*
   Address. Type style: Bodoni Black. Size: 9 points. Interline: 11 points.
   Information. Type style: Bodoni Black. Size: 10 points.

1

2

3

4

5

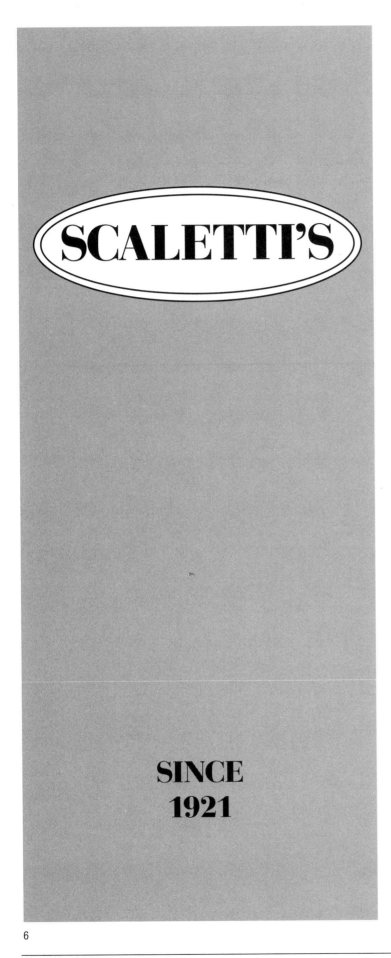

SINCE 1921

SCALETTI'S

Featuring
Northern Italian Specialties
Since 1921
Private Parties for 15 to 50
Valet Parking

—

(918)366-6241

228 Hudson Street, Bixby, Oklahoma
74008

SCALETTI'S

228 Hudson Street, Bixby, Oklahoma
74008
(918)366-6241

Quantity	Item	Cost
		Subtotal
		Tax
		Total

The Music Works logos have a musical quality because of the strong contrasts between the thick and thin strokes in Bodoni type styles.

Logos

1. *the.* Type style: Bodoni Black. Horizontal scale: 80%.
   MUSIC WORKS. Type style: Bodoni Poster slanted. Horizontal scale: 85%.
2. *the music.* Type style: Bodoni. Horizontal scale: 85%.
   WORKS. Type style: Bodoni Poster. Horizontal scale: 200%.
3. *the.* Type style: Bodoni Poster.
   MUSIC WORKS. Type style: Bodoni Black Condensed shadowed.
4. *the*. Type style: Bodoni Black Italic. Horizontal scale: 90%.
   MUSIC WORKS. Type style: Bodoni Black.
5. *the.* Type style: Bodoni Poster.
   Music. Type style: Bodoni Poster. Scale: Free form.
   WORKS. Type style: Bodoni Poster. Horizontal scale: 85%.

Applications

  Logo. THE MUSIC WORKS. Type style: Bodoni Poster.
6. **Letterhead.** (8.5x11) *Logo.*
   Tag line. Type style: Bodoni Black Italic. Size: 9 points.
   Name/Address. Type style: Bodoni Poster. Size: 9 points. Interline: 12 points.
7. **Repair Tag.** (4.5x2) *Logo.*
   Address/Information. Type style: Bodoni Poster. Size: 8 points.
   Phone. Type style: Bodoni Poster. Size: 12 points. Interline: 14 points.
8. **Business Card.** (2x3.5) *Logo.*
   Tag line. Type style: Bodoni Black Italic. Size: 9 points.
   Name/Address. Type style: Bodoni Poster. Size: 9 points. Interline: 12 points.
   Phone. Type style: Bodoni Poster. Size: 17 points.

1

the music

2

the MUSIC WORKS

3

the MUSIC WORKS

4

5

THE MUSIC WORKS

String and Band Instruments

**JOHN FISCHER
OWNER**

THE MUSIC WORKS

1463 COCHRANE AVE.
EL CAMINO, CA
91504

818/840-9286

Name	
Address	
Phone	
Repair	
Date Needed	

7

THE MUSIC WORKS

String and Band Instruments

1463 COCHRANE AVE.
EL CAMINO, CA
91504

818/840-9286

**JOHN FISCHER
OWNER**

8

1463 COCHRANE AVE.
EL CAMINO, CA
91504

6

This example shows how Bodoni can be modified to create a variety of condensed, expanded, outlined and reversed type styles that are reminiscent of nineteenth-century designs.

Logos

1. *Magic Man.* Type style: Bodoni Bold.
2. *Magic Man.* Type style: Bodoni Bold Condensed. Horizontal scale: 230%.
3. *Magic Man.* Type style: Bodoni Black. Horizontal scale: 20%.
4. *Magic Man.* Type style: Bodoni Poster outlined. Horizontal scale: 85%.
5. *magic man.* Typestyle: Bodoni Bold Italic.

Applications

Logo. Type style: Bodoni Poster. Horizontal scale: 85%.

6. **Letterhead.** (8.5x11) *Logo.*
   Features. Type style: Bodoni Poster. Size: 12 points. Interline: 15 points. Horizontal scale: 85%.
   Address/Phone. Type style: Bodoni Bold. Size: 11 points. Interline: 15 points. Horizontal scale: 85%.
7. **Business Card.** (3.5x2) *Logo.*
   Address/Name/Phone. Type style: Bodoni Bold. Size: 10 points. Interline: 15 points. Horizontal scale: 85%.
8. **Newspaper Ad.** (5x4) *Logo.*
   Features/Phone. Type style: Bodoni Poster. Size: 14 points. Interline: 18 points. Horizontal scale: 85%.
   Tag line. Type style: Bodoni Poster. Size: 16 points. Horizontal scale: 85%.
   Address. Type style: Bodoni Bold. Size: 8 points. Interline: 11 points. Horizontal scale: 85%.

1

2

3

4

5

Birthdays
Parties
Promotions
Banquets
Schools
Sales Meetings

509 Potomac Drive
Caldwell, ID 83605
208.342.0347

Magic Man

Barry Kimball, Professional Magician

7

Magic Man

Minor Mysteries to Illustrious Illusions

Birthdays
Parties
Promotions
Banquets
Schools
Sales Meetings

509 Potomac Drive
Caldwell, ID 83605

208.342.0347

8

Magic Man

509 Potomac Drive
Caldwell, ID 83605

208.342.0347

6

Bodoni

DeVors & Co. bookshop logo used in the applications is an interesting example of how Bodoni condensed to extreme proportions can be used to create a charming and distinctive image.

Logos

1. *DeVors/Co.* Type style: Bodoni Black.
   &. Type style: Bodoni Poster.
2. *DeVors/Co.* Type style: Bodoni Black Italic.
   &. Type style: Bodoni Bold Italic.
3. *DeVors & Co.* Type style: Bodoni Poster outlined. Horizontal scale: 150%.
4. *DeVors & Co.* Type style: Bodoni Black.

Applications

   Logo. *DeVors & Co.* Type style: Bodoni Black. Horizontal scale: 40%.
5. **Shopping Bag.** *Logo.*
6. **Business Card.** (3.5x2) *Logo.*
   Name/Tag line. Type style: Bodoni Black Italic. Size: 12 points.
   Address. Type style: Bodoni Black Italic. Size: 8 points.
7. **Sales Slip.** (5x7) *Logo.*
   Tag line. Type style: Bodoni Black. Size: 16 points.
   Address/Phone/Information. Type style: Bodoni Black. Size: 10 points.

1

2

3

4

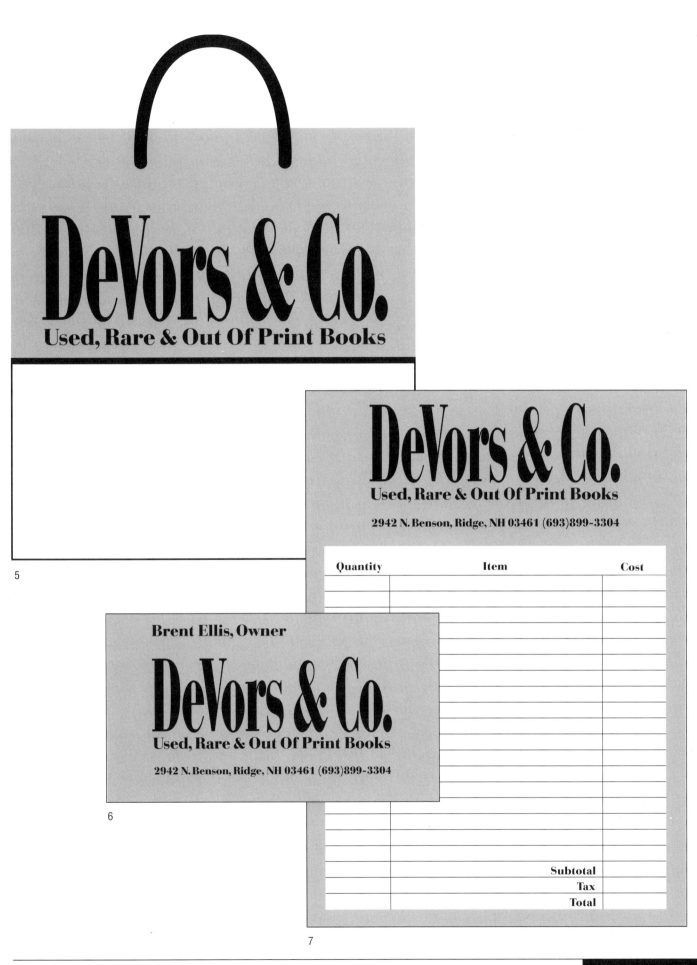

DeVors & Co.
Used, Rare & Out Of Print Books

5

DeVors & Co.
Used, Rare & Out Of Print Books

2942 N. Benson, Ridge, NH 03461 (693)899-3304

Quantity	Item	Cost
	Subtotal	
	Tax	
	Total	

Brent Ellis, Owner

DeVors & Co.
Used, Rare & Out Of Print Books

2942 N. Benson, Ridge, NH 03461 (693)899-3304

6

7

The Body Shop fitness center illustrates how to use Bookman to project a strong look with a personal charm.

Logos

1. *The Body Shop.* Type style: Bookman Demi.
2. *The/Shop.* Type style: Bookman Light. *BODY.* Type style: Bookman Demi Italic.
3. *The Body Shop.* Type style: Bookman Demi Italic outlined.
4. *The/Shop.* Type style: Bookman Light Italic. *BODY.* Type style: Bookman Demi. Horizontal scale: 70%.

Applications

Logo. The BODY Shop. Type style: Bookman Demi.
5. **Newspaper Ad.** (2.5x3) *Logo. Tag line/Services.* Type style: Bookman Demi. Size: 9 points. Interline: 12 points. *Phone.* Type style: Bookman Demi. Size: 15 points. *Address.* Type style: Bookman Light. Size: 9 points. Interline: 12 points.
6. **Business Card.** (3.5x2) *Logo. Tag line.* Type style: Bookman Demi. Size: 12 points. *Address.* Type style: Bookman Light. Size: 9 points. Interline: 12 points. *Name/Phone.* Type style: Bookman Demi. Size: 9 points.
7. **T-Shirt.** *Logo.*

The Body Shop

1

The
BODY
Shop

2

The Body Shop

3

THE
BODY
SHOP

4

The **BODY** Shop

Personalized Body Building Programs

Nutrition Counseling
Free Weights
Universal
Massage

509-475-4133

8432 Becker Road
Yakima, Washington 98903

5

The **BODY** Shop

For a Total Tune-Up

The **BODY** Shop

Personalized Body Building Programs

8432 Becker Road
Yakima, Washington 98903
509-475-4133

Gary Davis, Fitness Consultant

6

7

The use of capitals and centered composition forms an identity of old-fashioned reliability and craftsmanship for the Hamlin Construction Company.

Logos

1. *hamlin.* Type style: Bookman Demi. **CONSTRUCTION CO.** Type style: Bookman Light. Horizontal scale: 70%.
2. *HAMLIN.* Type style: Bookman Demi Italic. **CONSTRUCTION CO.** Type style: Bookman Light.
3. *HAMLIN.* Type style: Bookman Demi. Horizontal scale: 70%. **CONSTRUCTION CO.** Type style: Bookman Light.
4. *hamlin.* Type style: Bookman Demi. **CONSTRUCTION CO.** Type style: Bookman Light.

Applications

   Logo. *HAMLIN.* Type style: Bookman Demi. **CONSTRUCTION CO.** Type style: Bookman Light.
5. **Job Estimate.** *Logo.* *Tag line/Address.* Type style: Bookman. Size: 8 points. Horizontal scale: 90%. *Phone.* Type style: Bookman Demi. Size: 11 points. Horizontal scale: 90%. *Information.* Type style: Bookman Demi. Size: 10 points. Interline: 13 points. Horizontal scale: 90%.
6. **Business Card.** (3.5x2) *Logo.* *Tag line/Address.* Type style: Bookman. Size: 8 points. Horizontal scale: 90%. *Phone/Name.* Type style: Bookman Demi. Size: 11 points. Interline: 13 points. Horizontal scale: 90%.
7. **Van.** *Logo.*

hamlin
CONSTRUCTION CO.

1

HAMLIN
CONSTRUCTION CO.

2

HAMLIN
CONSTRUCTION CO.

3

hamlin

CONSTRUCTION CO.

4

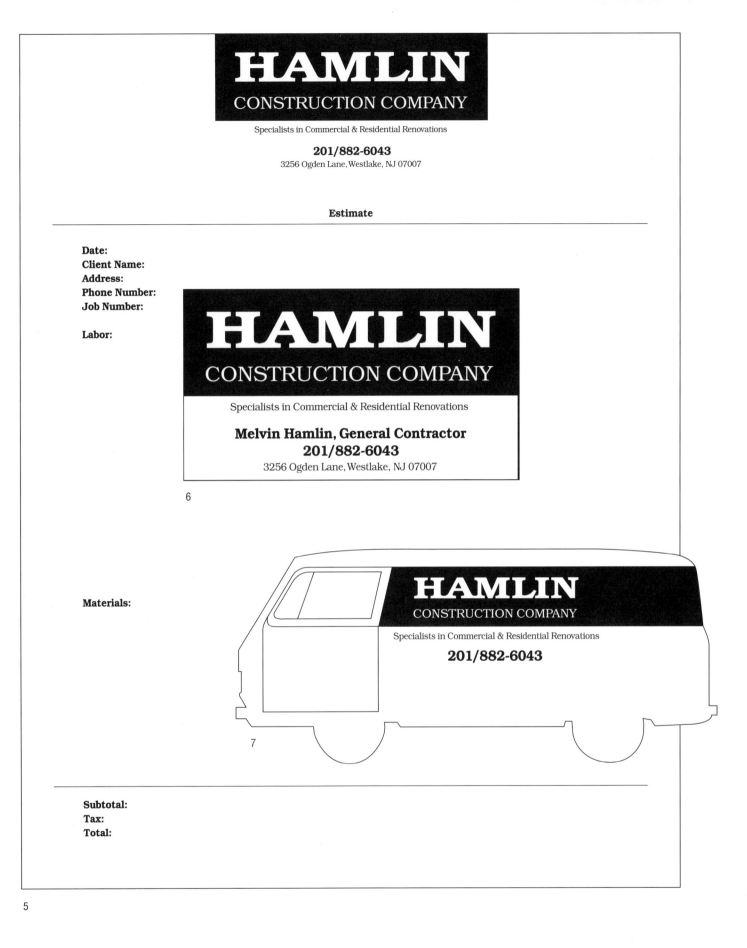

HAMLIN
CONSTRUCTION COMPANY

Specialists in Commercial & Residential Renovations

201/882-6043
3256 Ogden Lane, Westlake, NJ 07007

Estimate

Date:
Client Name:
Address:
Phone Number:
Job Number:

Labor:

HAMLIN
CONSTRUCTION COMPANY

Specialists in Commercial & Residential Renovations

Melvin Hamlin, General Contractor
201/882-6043
3256 Ogden Lane, Westlake, NJ 07007

6

Materials:

HAMLIN
CONSTRUCTION COMPANY

Specialists in Commercial & Residential Renovations

201/882-6043

7

Subtotal:
Tax:
Total:

5

Using Bookman to develop a logo for The Music Works store produces a "no frills" image that suggests straightforward value and service. Note how well Bookman and Bookman Demi adapt to free-form manipulation in logo 3.

Logos

1. *The.* Type style: Bookman Light Italic.
   MUSIC WORKS. Type style: Bookman Demi Italic.
2. *the.* Type style: Bookman Demi.
   MUSIC WORKS. Type style: Bookman Demi. Horizontal scale: 65%.
3. *the/Works.* Type style: Bookman Demi outlined.
   Music. Type style: Bookman Demi. Scale: Free form.
4. *The.* Type style: Bookman Light.
   MUSIC WORKS. Type style: Bookman Light Italic. Horizontal scale: 150%.
5. *The Music.* Type style: Bookman Light. Horizontal scale: 85%.
   WORKS. Type style: Bookman Demi. Horizontal scale: 90%.

Applications

Logo. *The Music Works.* Type style: Bookman Demi.
6. **Newspaper Ad.** (5x6.25) *Logo.*
   Tag line. Type style: Bookman Light. Size: 28 points. Interline: 28 points.
   Services. Type style: Bookman Demi. Size: 20 points. Interline: 24 points.
   Phone/Address. Type style: Bookman Light. Size: 16 points. Interline: 19 points.
7. **Business Card.** (2x3.5) *Logo.*
   Tag line. Type style: Bookman Light. Size: 14 points. Interline: 14 points.
   Name/Phone. Type style: Bookman Demi. Size: 12 points.
   Owner/Address. Type style: Bookman Light. Size: 10 points. Interline: 13 points.
8. **Repair Tag.** (4.5x2) *Logo.*
   Tag line. Type style: Bookman Light. Size: 9 points. Interline: 9 points.
   Phone. Type style: Bookman Demi. Size: 9 points.
   Information. Type style: Bookman Light. Size: 8 points.

1

2

3

4

5

The Music WORKS

String & Band Instruments

SOLD

REPAIRED

EXCHANGED

RENTED

818-840-9286

1463 Cochrane Ave., El Camino, CA 91504

6

The Music WORKS

String & Band Instruments

John Fischer

Owner

818-840-9286

1463 Cochrane Ave.
El Camino, CA 91504

7

The Music WORKS

String & Band Instruments

818-840-9286

NAME	
PHONE	
REPAIR	
DATE	
DATE NEEDED	

8

Top Notch Tree service demonstrates how Bookman Bold can be used to symbolically suggest a tree through the use of a large initial capital letter.

Logos

1. ***Top NOTCH.*** Type style: Bookman Light.
2. ***Top Notch.*** Type style: Bookman Demi Italic.
3. ***T.*** Type style: Bookman Demi.
   Top notch. Type style: Bookman Light Italic.
4. ***top.*** Type style: Bookman Demi outlined.
   notch. Type style: Bookman Demi.
5. ***TOP.*** Type style: Bookman Light. Horizontal scale: 150%.
   NOTCH. Type style: Bookman Light.

Applications

   Logo. *T.* Type style: Bookman Demi.
   Top notch. Type style: Bookman Light.
6. **Business Card.** (3.5x2) ***Logo.***
   Phone/Tag line/Name. Type style: Bookman Demi. Size: 10 points. Interline: 12 points.
   Address. Type style: Bookman Light. Size: 8 points. Interline: 10 points.
7. **Newspaper Ad.** (2.5x6.25) ***Logo.***
   Tag line. Type style: Bookman Demi. Size: 8 points. Interline: 10 points.
   Services. Type style: Bookman Demi. Size: 11 points. Interline: 13 points.
   Phone/Address. Type style: Bookman Light. Size: 11 points. Interline: 13 points.
8. **Truck. *Logo.***

1

2

3

4

5

Top notch

Tree Trimming
and Stump Removal

Fully Insured
Free Estimates

(201)347-5561

Year-Round
Citywide
and Suburban
Services

72 Howe Street
Corley, NJ 07032

7

(201)347-5561

Top notch

Tree Trimming
and Stump Removal

72 Howe Street
Corley, NJ 07032

Jim Clark, Owner

6

Top notch

Tree Trimming
and Stump Removal

(201)347-5561

8

The Holistic Health Center is used to show how Bookman can be used to convey a natural and personal look for a health service company.

Logos

1. *Holistic.* Type style: Bookman Light. *Health Center.* Type style: Bookman Demi.
2. *Holistic Health Center.* Type style: Bookman Light Italic.
3. *HOLISTIC.* Type style: Bookman Light. *HEALTH CENTER.* Type style: Bookman Demi.
4. *H.* Type style: Bookman Demi outlined. *Holistic Health Center.* Type style: Bookman Light Italic.

Applications

Logo. *HOLISTIC.* Type style: Bookman Demi. *HEALTH CENTER.* Type style: Bookman Light.

5. **Building Sign.** *Logo.*
6. **Business Card.** (2x3.5) *Logo.* *Tag line/Name.* Type style: Bookman Demi. Size: 11 points. Interline: 14 points. *Address.* Type style: Bookman Light. Size: 10 points. Interline: 13 points.
7. **Envelope.** (#10 business) *Logo.* *Tag line.* Type style: Bookman Demi. Size: 10 points. Interline: 12 points. *Address/Phone.* Type style: Bookman Light. Size: 9 points. Interline: 12 points.

Holistic
Health Center

1

Holistic

2

Health Center

3

4

HOLISTIC
HEALTH CENTER
Specialized
Preventative Medicine

5

6

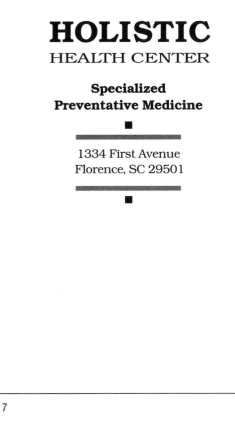

7

The type designs for the law firm of Anson C. Borst and Associates emphasize the timeless character of Caslon type composed with centered alignment.

Logos

1. ***Anson C. Borst and Associates.*** Type style: Caslon 540. Horizontal scale: 85%.
2. ***Anson C. Borst and Associates.*** Type style: Caslon 540. Horizontal scale: 85%.
3. ***A.*** Type style: Caslon 3 Italic. Horizontal scale: 85%.
   Anson C. Borst and Associates. Type style: Caslon 540 Italic. Horizontal scale: 85%.
4. ***A.*** Type style: Caslon 540. Horizontal scale: 85%.
   Anson C. Borst and Associates. Type style: Caslon 3 Italic. Horizontal scale: 85%.

Applications

Logo. ***Anson C. Borst/Associates.*** Type style: Caslon 3.
and. Type style: Caslon 540 Italic.

5. **Invoice.** (8.5x11) ***Logo.***
   Tag line/Phone/Services. Type style: Caslon 540. Size: 11 points. Interline: 14 points.
   Address. Type style: Caslon 540. Size: 9 points.
6. **Business Card.** (3.5x2) ***Logo.***
   Tag line/Phone/Name. Type style: Caslon 540. Size: 11 points. Interline: 13 points.
   Address. Type style: Caslon 540. Size: 9 points.
7. **Envelope.** (#10 business) ***Logo.***
   Tag line. Type style: Caslon 540. Size: 10 points.
   Address. Type style: Caslon 540. Size: 8 points.

Anson C. Borst and Associates

1

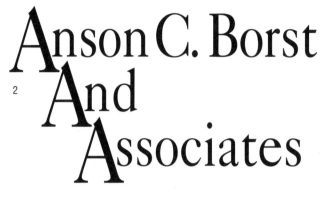

2

3

4

Anson C. Borst *and* **Associates**

Personal Injury and Medical Malpractice

413-536-1429

Brandeis Center, Suite 938, Chicopee, MA 01013

Invoice

Date:
Client Number:
Matter Number:

_____

Anson C. Borst *and* **Associates**

Personal Injury and Medical Malpractice

Anson C. Borst *and* **Associates**

Personal Injury and Medical Malpractice

Michael Krell, Esq.
413-536-1429

Brandeis Center, Suite 938, Chicopee, MA 01013

5

Brandeis Center, Suite 938, Chicopee, MA 01013

7

_____

Total

6

These examples for Off the Cuff vintage evening wear demonstrate how you can horizontally scale Caslon and retain the classic image of the business.

Logos

1. ***Off the Cuff.*** Type style: Caslon 3 Italic.
2. ***Off.*** Type style: Caslon 3 Italic. Horizontal scale: 70%.
   the Cuff. Type style: Caslon 3 Italic slanted. Horizontal scale: 60%.
3. ***Off/Cuff.*** Type style: Caslon 3.
   the. Type style: Caslon 540.
4. ***OFF THE CUFF.*** Type style: Caslon 540.
5. ***OFF/CUFF.*** Type style: Caslon 3 Italic.
   the. Type style: Caslon 540 Italic.

Applications

   Logo. Type style: Caslon 3. Horizontal scale: 150%.
6. **Letterhead.** (8.5x11) ***Logo.***
   Tag line. Type style: Caslon 3. Size: 12 points.
   Address. Type style: Caslon 540. Size: 10 points. Interline: 12 points.
7. **Business Card.** (2x3.5) ***Logo.***
   Tag line/Name/Phone. Type style: Caslon 3. Size: 12 points.
   Address/Title. Type style: Caslon 540. Size: 10 points. Interline: 12 points.
8. **Product Tag.** (2x4.25) ***Logo.***
   Tag line/Size/Cost. Type style: Caslon 3. Size: 12 points. Interline: 15 points.
   Information. Type style: Caslon 540. Size: 9 points. Interline: 11 points.
9. **Newspaper Ad.** (2.5x3) ***Logo.***
   Tag line/Phone. Type style: Caslon 3. Size: 15 points.
   Services/Address. Type style: Caslon 540. Size: 10 points. Interline: 12 points.

1

2

3

4

5

OFF
THE
CUFF
Vintage Evening Wear

OFF
THE
CUFF
Vintage Evening Wear

Beaded Dresses, Furs, Accessories
(804) 627-3681

1104 Seneca Ave.
Norfolk, Virginia
23516

9

OFF
THE
CUFF
Vintage Evening Wear

Item No.
Code No.

Size
Cost

8

OFF
THE
CUFF
Vintage Evening Wear

1104 Seneca Ave.
Norfolk, Virginia
23516

Blair Jamieson
Owner
(804) 627-3681

6

1104 Seneca Ave.
Norfolk, Virginia
23516

7

The logos for Down the Aisle wedding consultants show how Caslon can be used to create an image of reliability and trust.

Logos

1. **Down the Aisle.** Type style: Caslon 3 Italic.
2. **down the Aisle.** Type style: Caslon 540 Italic.
   A. Type style: Caslon 3. Horizontal scale: 150%.
3. **Down the Aisle.** Type style: Caslon 540. Horizonal scale: 85%.
4. **Down the Aisle.** Type style: Caslon 540.
   A. Type style: Caslon 540 outlined.
5. **D.** Type style: Caslon 3 Italic outlined.
   Down the Aisle. Type style: Caslon 3 Italic.

Applications

Logo. Down the Aisle. Type style: Caslon 540.

6. **Letterhead.** (8.5x11) **Logo.**
   Tag line. Type style: Caslon 3. Size: 9 points. Interline: 11 points.
   Address. Type style: Caslon 540. Size: 8 points. Interline: 11 points.
7. **Envelope.** (#10 business) **Logo.**
   Tag line. Type style: Caslon 3. Size: 9 points. Interline: 11 points.
   Address. Type style: Caslon 540. Size: 8 points. Interline: 11 points.
8. **Business Card.** (2x3.5) **Logo.**
   Tag line. Type style: Caslon 3. Size: 9 points. Interline: 11 points.
   Name. Type style: Caslon 3. Size: 14 points.
   Title/Address. Type style: Caslon 540. Size: 8 points. Interline: 11 points.

Down the Aisle

1

down the A*isle*

2

D*o*wn the Aisle

3

Down the A*isle*

4

Down the Aisle

5

Down
the
Aisle

Complete Wedding
Services

Down
the
Aisle

Complete Wedding
Services

312 W. Eastland Road, Parker, WV
26201

7

Down
the
Aisle

Complete Wedding
Services

Rose Selkin

Wedding Consultant

(304) 472-4600
312 W. Eastland Road, Parker, WV
26201

8

(304) 472-4600
312 W. Eastland Road, Parker, WV
26201

6

Various DeVors & Co. logos demonstrate Caslon's decorative side as illustrated by the italics and the italic ampersand.

Logos

1. *DeVors & Co.* Type style: Caslon 540.
2. *DeVors & Co.* Type style: Caslon 3 outlined. Horizontal scale: 150%.
3. *DeVors & Co.* Type style: Caslon 540 Italic.
4. *DeVors & Co.* Type style: Caslon 3. Horizontal scale: 70%.
5. *DeVors/Co.* Type style: Caslon 540. *&.* Type style: Caslon 540 Italic.

Applications

Logo. *DeVors/Co.* Type style: Caslon 3. *&.* Type style: Caslon 540 Italic.

6. Envelope. (#10 business) *Logo.*
Tag line. Type style: Caslon 3. Size: 12 points.
Address. Type style: Caslon 540. Size: 9 points.

7. Sales Slip. (5x7) *Logo.*
Tag line. Type style: Caslon 3. Size: 18 points.
Address/Phone. Type style: Caslon 540. Size: 12 points. Interline: 15 points.
Information. Type style: Caslon 3. Size: 12 points. Interline: 15 points.

8. Business Card. (3.5x2) *Logo.*
Tag line. Type style: Caslon 3. Size: 13 points.
Address/Phone/Name. Type style: Caslon 540. Size: 10 points. Interline: 12 points.

1

2

3

4

5

DeVors&Co.

Used, Rare and Out Of Print Books

2942 N. Benson, Ridge, NH 03461

6

DeVors&Co.

Used, Rare and Out Of Print Books

2942 N. Benson, Ridge, NH 03461
693-899-3304

Quantity	Item	Cost
	Subtotal	
	Tax	
	Total	

7

DeVors&Co.

Used, Rare and Out Of Print Books

2942 N. Benson, Ridge, NH 03461
693-899-3304
Brent Ellis, Owner

8

The logos for the Ariel String Quartet display the illustrative qualities of Caslon by integrating the type and the symbolic line elements that suggest strings.

Logos

1. *ARIEL.* Type style: Caslon 3. Horizontal scale: 150%.
   STRING. Type style: Caslon 3. Horizontal scale: 220%.
   QUARTET. Type style: Caslon 3. Horizontal scale: 80%.
2. *ARIEL.* Type style: Caslon 3. Horizontal scale: 130%.
   STRING QUARTET. Type style: Caslon 3. Horizontal scale: 80%.
3. *ARIEL.* Type style: Caslon 3. Horizontal scale: 150%.
   STRING. Type style: Caslon 3. Horizontal scale: 220%.
   QUARTET. Type style: Caslon 3. Horizontal scale: 80%.
4. *Ariel String Quartet.* Type style: Caslon 540.

Applications

   Logo. *Ariel String Quartet.* Type style: Caslon 3.
5. **Letterhead.** (8.5x11) *Logo.*
   Tag line/Address/Phone. Type style: Caslon 540. Size: 11 points. Interline: 14 points.
6. **Program Cover.** (11x8.5) *Logo.*
   Name/Title/Features. Type style: Caslon 540. Size: 24 points.
7. **Business Card.** (2x3.5) *Logo.*
   Name/Title. Type style: Caslon 540. Size: 11 points. Interline: 14 points.
   Tag line/Address/Phone. Type style: Caslon 540. Size: 8 points. Interline: 12 points.
8. **Envelope.** (#10 business) *Logo.*
   Tag line/Address. Type style: Caslon 540. Size: 11 points. Interline: 14 points.

1

2

3

4

Ariel
String Quartet

Represented by
Harlan Holt Limited

Ariel
String Quartet

Dr. Peter Jansen
Violist

Represented by Harlan Holt Limited
164 West 57th Street
New York, New York 59601
(212) 841-9514

7

Ariel
String Quartet

Beethoven

Brahms

Haydn

Dr. Peter Jansen, Violist

6

Ariel
String Quartet

Represented by
Harlan Holt Limited

164 West 57th Street
New York, New York 59601

8

164 West 57th Street
New York, New York 59601

(212) 841-9514

5

The Music Works logo exemplifies how Frutiger can be used to illustrate music symbols such as notes. Other examples demonstrate the rhythmic letterform distortions that relate to musical sounds.

Logos

1. *the.* Type style: Frutiger 55.
   Music. Type style: Frutiger 85.
   WORKS. Type style: Frutiger 85.
   Horizontal scale: 65%.
2. *the music.* Type style: Frutiger 55.
   Horizontal scale: 70%.
   WORKS. Type style: Frutiger 85.
   Horizontal scale: 170%.
3. *the.* Type style: Frutiger 45. Horizontal scale: 125%.
   MUSIC WORKS. Type style: Frutiger 75 outlined and shadowed. Horizontal scale: 70%.
4. *the.* Type style: Frutiger 45. Horizontal scale: 80%.
   Music. Type style: Frutiger 85. Scale: Free form.
   WORKS. Type style: Frutiger 85. Horizontal scale: 75%.
5. *the.* Type style: Frutiger 45. Horizontal scale: 70%.
   MUSIC WORKS. Frutiger 75 outlined and shadowed. Horizontal scale: 80%.

Applications

Logo. *the.* Type style: Frutiger 45. Horizontal scale: 50%.
MUSIC WORKS. Type style: Frutiger 85. Horizontal scale: 250%.
6. **Letterhead.** (8.5x11) *Logo.*
   Address/Phone. Type style: Frutiger 55. Size: 8 points. Interline: 11 points.
7. **Sales Slip.** (8.5x11) *Logo.*
   Items. Type style: Frutiger 65. Size: 12 points.
   Address/Phone. Type style: Frutiger 55. Size: 8 points. Interline: 11 points.
8. **Business Card.** (3.5x2) *Logo.*
   Name. Type style: Frutiger 65. Size: 9 points.
   Title/Address/Phone. Type style: Frutiger 55. Size: 8 points. Interline: 11 points.

1

the music

2

3

4

5

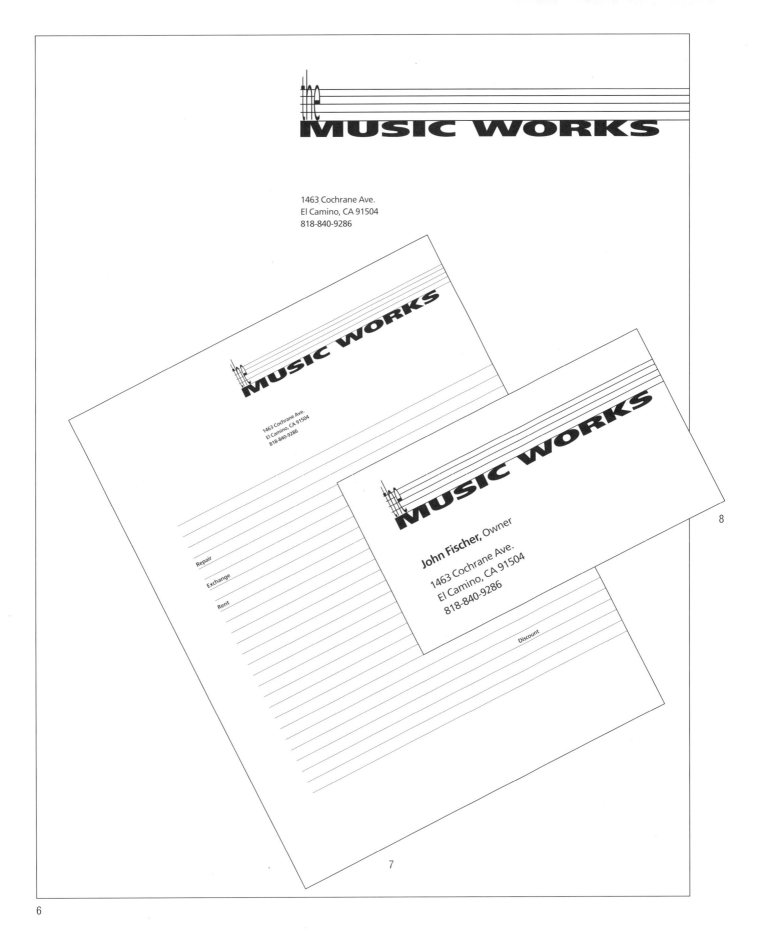

Odilon, a contemporary apparel shop, gives us an opportunity to use Frutiger to create a stylish image through the distortion and repetition of the letterforms.

Logos

1. *O.* Type style: Frutiger 75.
    ODILON. Type style: Frutiger 75. Scale: Free form.
    ODILON. Type style: Frutiger 55. Scale: Free form.
2. *ODILON.* Type style: Frutiger 75. Horizontal scale: 50%.
3. *ODILON.* Type style: Frutiger 75. Baseline: Free form curve.
4. *Odilon.* Type style: Frutiger 85. Horizontal scale: 225%. Effect: Mirrored and shadowed.
5. *O.* Type style: Frutiger 85. Horizontal scale: 50%.
    odilon. Type style: Frutiger 85 oblique. Horizontal scale: 60%.
6. *O.* Type style: Frutiger 85 oblique. Horizontal scale: 50%.
    odilon. Type style: Frutiger 75. Horizontal scale: 60%.
7. *O.* Type style: Frutiger 55. Horizontal scale: 50%.
    odilon. Type style: Frutiger 85. Horizontal scale: 60%.
8. *Odilon.* Type style: Frutiger 85. Horizontal scale: 200%. Effect: shadow.
9. *Odilon.* Type style: Frutiger 85. Horizontal scale: 200%. Effect: shadow.

Applications

  Logo. Odilon. Type style: Frutiger 85. Horizontal scale: 275%.
10. **Newspaper Ad.** (5x6.25) *Logo.*
    Headline. Type style: Frutiger 65. Size: 24 points.
    Features/Phone. Type style: Frutiger 65. Size: 14 points.
    Address. Type style: Frutiger 65. Size: 10 points.
11. **Price Tag.** *Logo.*
    Information. Type style: Frutiger 65. Size: 14 points.
12. **Wrapping Paper.** *Logo.* Effect: repeated pattern.

1

2

3

4

5

6

7

8

9

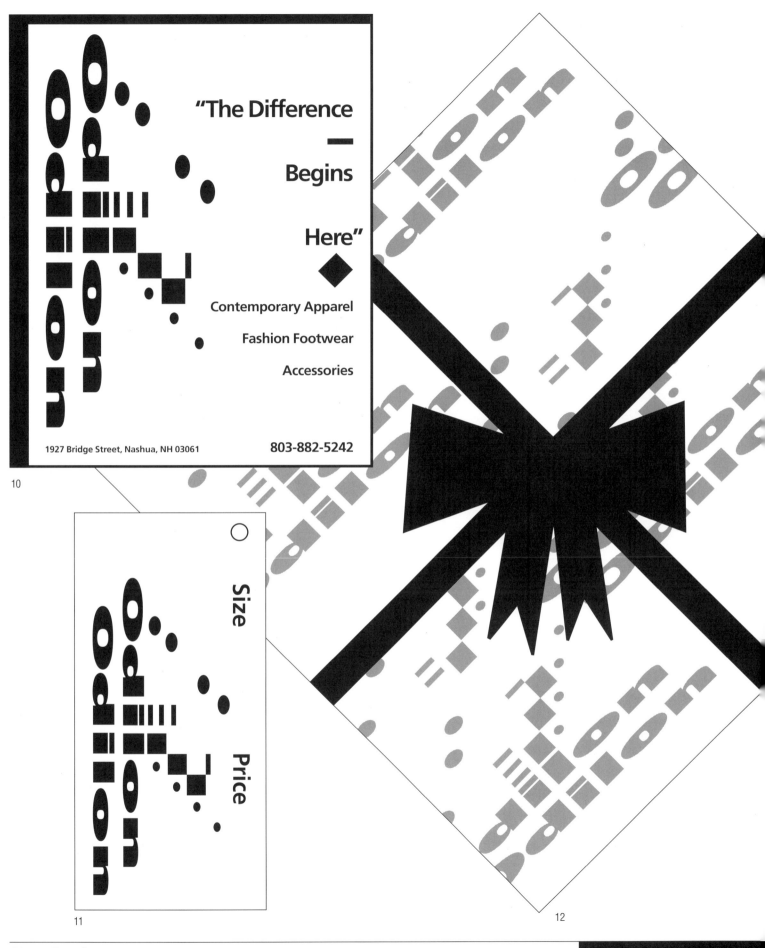

"The Difference
—
Begins

Here"

Contemporary Apparel

Fashion Footwear

Accessories

1927 Bridge Street, Nashua, NH 03061

803-882-5242

10

11

Size

Price

12

Frutiger

Frutiger lends itself to symbolic representation of cat eyes and tiger stripes in these examples for the Tigger Too toy store.

Logos

1. *TT.* Type style: Frutiger 85. Scale: Free form.
   Tigger Too. Type style: Frutiger 85. Horizontal scale: 70%.
2. *TIGGER TOO.* Type style: Frutiger 75. Baseline: Curved.
   TT. Type style: Frutiger 85. Horizontal scale: 200%.
   O. Type style: Frutiger 85. Horizontal scale: 500%.
3. *TIGGER TOO.* Type style: Frutiger 85.
4. *TIGGER TOO.* Type style: Frutiger 85.
   TT. Type style: Frutiger 85. Scale: Free form.
5. *TIGGER TOO.* Type style: Frutiger 45. Horizontal scale: 60%. Effect: Shadow.
   OO. Type style: Frutiger 85. Horizontal scale: 60%. Effect: Shadow.

Applications

Logo. *T.* Type style: Frutiger 85. Scale: Free form.
Tigger Too. Type style: Frutiger 85. Horizontal scale: 90%.

6. **Ad.** (5x6.25) *Logo.*
   Headline/Phone. Type style: Frutiger 75. Size: 18 points. Horizontal scale: 85%.
   Address. Type style: Frutiger 55. Size: 9 points.
7. **Business Card.** (3.5x2) *Logo.*
   Name. Type style: Frutiger 75. Size: 9 points.
   Address/Phone/Title. Type style: Frutiger 55. Size: 8 points. Interline: 11 points.
8. **Envelope.** (#10 business) *Logo.*
   Address. Type style: Frutiger 55. Size: 10 points. Interline: 13 points.

1

2

3

4

5

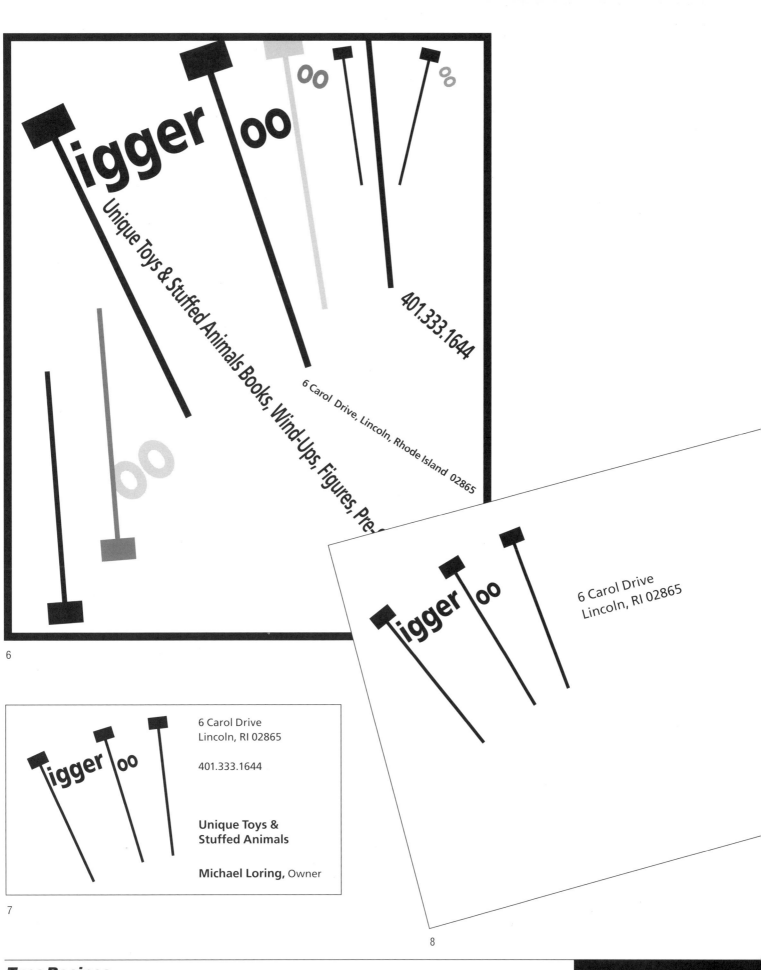

Tigger Too

Unique Toys & Stuffed Animals Books, Wind-Ups, Figures, Pre...

401.333.1644

6 Carol Drive, Lincoln, Rhode Island 02865

6

Tigger Too

6 Carol Drive
Lincoln, RI 02865

401.333.1644

**Unique Toys &
Stuffed Animals**

Michael Loring, Owner

7

Tigger Too

6 Carol Drive
Lincoln, RI 02865

8

The logos for the Magic Man magician emphasize how Frutiger can be used to create distortions that are mysterious and dramatic.

Special Effects

1. *Magic Man.* Type style: Frutiger 85 outlined. Scale: Free form.
2. *MM.* Type style: Frutiger 85. Scale: Free form.
   Magic Man. Type style: Frutiger 85. Horizontal scale: 130%.
3. *MAGIC MAN.* Type style: Frutiger 85 outlined. Horizontal scale: 70%.
4. *Magic Man.* Type style: Frutiger 65. Horizontal scale: 90%.
   Magic Man. Frutiger 65 outlined. Scale: Free form.

Applications

Logo. *M.* Type style: Frutiger 85. *Magic Man.* Frutiger 75. Horizontal scale: 90%.

5. **Letterhead.** (8.5x11) *Logo.*
   Tag line/Phone. Type style: Frutiger 65. Size: 10 points. Interline: 14 points.
   Address. Type style: Frutiger 55. Size: 9 points. Interline: 13 points.
6. **Newspaper Ad.** (5x6) *Logo.*
   Headline. Type style: Frutiger 85. Size: 24 points. Horizontal scale: 85%.
   Features/Name/Phone. Type style: Frutiger 65. Size: 10 points. Interline: 14 points.
   Title/Address. Type style: Frutiger 55. Size: 9 points. Interline: 13 points.
7. **Business Card.** (3.5x2) *Logo.*
   Name/Phone. Type style: Frutiger 65. Size: 10 points.
   Title/Address. Type style: Frutiger 55. Size: 8 points. Interline: 11 points.

1

2

3

4

Minor Mysteries to Illustrious Illusions

Birthdays
Parties
Promotions
Banquets
Schools
Sales Meetings

Magic Man

Barry Kimball
Professional Magician

509 Potomac Drive
Caldwell, ID 83605
208.342.0347

6

**Minor Mysteries to
Illustrious Illusions**

509 Potomac Drive
Caldwell, ID 83605

208.342.0347

5

Barry Kimball

Professional Magician

509 Potomac Drive
Caldwell, ID 83605

208.342.0347

7

Frutiger

Scaletti's Italian restaurant demonstrates how to create symbolic representations with type, as pasta and a checkered table-cloth pattern.

Logos

1. **S.** Type style: Frutiger 85.
   Scaletti's. Type style: Frutiger 85.
   Horizontal scale: 240%.
2. **S.** Type style: Frutiger 75 outlined.
   scaletti's. Type style: Frutiger 75.
   Horizontal scale: 150%.
3. **S.** Type style: Frutiger 75. Horizontal
   scale: 60%.
   Scaletti's. Type style: Frutiger 75.
4. **SCALETTI'S.** Type style: Frutiger 85.
   Horizontal scale: 60%.
   S. Type style: Frutiger 55 outlined.

Applications

   Logo. Type style: Frutiger 85. Horizontal
   scale: 90%.
5. **Menu.** (6.75x17) *Logo.*
   Tag line. Frutiger. Size: 36 points.
6. **Newspaper Ad.** (2.5x4.25) *Logo.*
   Headline/Phone. Type style: Frutiger
   65. Size: 18 points. Interline: 22 points.
   Information/Address. Type style:
   Frutiger 65. Size: 10 points. Interline:
   12 points.
7. **Customer Check.** (4.25x5.5) *Logo.*
   Information. Type style: Frutiger 65.
   Size: 10 points. Interline: 24 points.

1

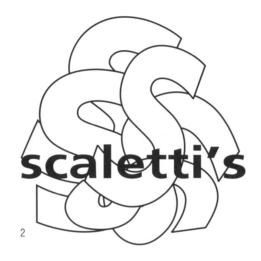

2

3

4

SCALETTI'S

Featuring
Northern
Italian
Specialties
Since 1931

5

SCALETTI'S

A Beautiful New Look for the City's
Oldest Italian Restaurant

Featuring Northern Italian Specialties

Serving Lunch, Dinner and Cocktails
Private Parties for 15 to 50
All major Credit Cards
For Reservations Call

918-366-6241

228 Hudson Street, Bixby, Oklahoma

6

SCALETTI'S

Server No.	No. Persons
Date	Table No.

	Subtotal
	Tax
	Total

7

Sky Wheels airport taxi service demonstrates how the use of outlined and slanted Helvetica Condensed can be used to show speed, motion and flight.

Logos

1. *Sky Wheels.* Type style: Helvetica Ultra Compressed. Oblique: 18 degrees.
2. **SKY WHEELS.** Type style: Helvetica Extra Compressed outlined. Horizontal scale: 250%.
3. **SKY WHEELS.** Type style: Helvetica Ultra Compressed.
4. *Sky Wheels.* Type style: Helvetica Ultra Compressed.
5. *Sky.* Type style: Helvetica Condensed Black Oblique.
   WHEELS. Type style: Helvetica Bold Oblique.

Applications

Logo. *Sky.* Type style: Helvetica Extra Compressed outlined. Horizontal scale: 250%.
Wheels. Type style: Helvetica Condensed Black Oblique.

6. **Ad.** (2.5x6.25) *Logo.*
   Headline. Type style: Helvetica Black Oblique. Size: 19 points. *Phone.* Type style: Helvetica Black Oblique. Size: 23 points. *Address.* Type style: Helvetica Condensed Light. Size: 9 points.
   Services. Type style: Helvetica Condensed Light. Size: 13 points. Interline: 16 points.
7. **Ad.** (2.5x3) *Logo.*
   Phone. Type style: Helvetica Black Oblique. Size: 21 points. *Address.* Type style: Helvetica Condensed Light. Size: 8 points. *Headline.* Type style: Helvetica Black Oblique. Size: 12 points.
   Services. Type style: Helvetica Condensed. Size: 12 points.
8. **Business Card.** (3.5x2) *Logo.*
   Services/Address. Type style: Helvetica Condensed Light. Size: 9 points. Interline: 11 points. *Phone.* Type style: Helvetica Condensed Black Oblique. Size: 23 points.
9. **Taxi.** *Logo.*

1

2

3

4

5

SKY WHEELS

We Deliver On Time

301-685-0692
2749 Turner Lane, Baltimore, MD 21201

24-Hour Radio Dispatch
Special Airport Service
Fast Service
Citywide

6

SKY WHEELS

301-685-0692
2749 Turner Lane, Baltimore, MD 21201

We Deliver On Time

24-Hour Radio Dispatch
Special Airport Service
Fast Service
Citywide

7

SKY WHEELS

Citywide Special Airport Service
24-Hour Radio Dispatch

301-685-0692

2749 Turner Lane, Baltimore, MD 21201

8

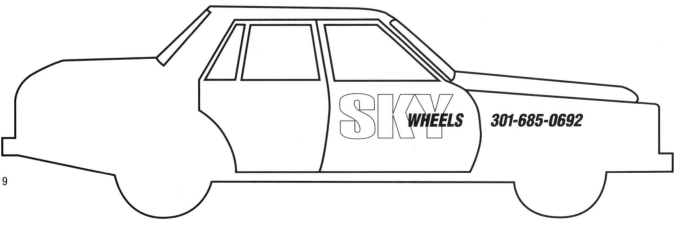

SKY WHEELS 301-685-0692

9

The Hamlin Construction Company illustrates how Helvetica Condensed and Compressed type styles can be manipulated to present a personable yet rugged mechanical image.

Logos

1. *hamlin.* Type style: Helvetica Extra Compressed. Horizontal scale: 200%. *CONSTRUCTION CO.* Type style: Helvetica Condensed Bold Oblique.
2. *hamlin.* Type style: Helvetica Extra Compressed. Horizontal scale: 200%. *CONSTRUCTION CO.* Type style: Helvetica Condensed.
3. *HAMLIN.* Type style: Helvetica Condensed Bold Oblique. Horizontal scale: 200%. *CONSTRUCTION CO.* Type style: Helvetica Condensed.
4. *H.* Type style: Helvetica Compressed outlined. *HAMLIN.* Type style: Helvetica Extra Compressed. Horizontal scale: 200%. *CONSTRUCTION CO.* Type style: Helvetica Condensed Light.

Applications

    Logo. *hamlin.* Type style: Helvetica Ultra Compressed. Oblique: 18 degrees. *CONSTRUCTION CO.* Type style: Helvetica Condensed Light Oblique.
5. **Van.** *Logo.*
6. **Ad.** (4x5) *Logo. Tag line.* Type style: Helvetica Condensed Bold Oblique. Size: 12 points. Interline: 14 points. *Address.* Type style: Helvetica Condensed Light Oblique. Size: 12 points. Interline: 14 points. *Phone.* Type style: Helvetica Condensed Bold Oblique. Size: 12 points.
7. **Envelope.** (#10 business) *Logo. Tag line.* Type style: Helvetica Condensed Bold Oblique. Size: 9 points. Interline: 12 points. *Address.* Type style: Helvetica Condensed Light Oblique. Size: 8 points. Interline: 12 points.
8. **Business Card.** (3x2.5) *Logo. Tag line/Name.* Type style: Helvetica Condensed Bold Oblique. Size: 9 points. Interline: 12 points. *Address/Phone/Title.* Type style: Helvetica Condensed Light Oblique. Size: 8 points. Interline: 12 points.

1

CONSTRUCTION CO.

2

3

4

5

6

7

8

The Holistic Health Center shows how Helvetica Condensed type styles can be used to create a clean, orderly and personal image.

Logos

1. *Holistic Health.* Type style: Helvetica Condensed Light.
   Center. Type style: Helvetica Condensed Black.
2. *HOLISTIC/CENTER.* Type style: Helvetica Ultra Compressed.
   HEALTH. Type style: Helvetica Extra Compressed outlined. Horizontal scale: 300%.
3. *HOLISTIC/CENTER.* Type style: Helvetica Condensed Black.
   HEALTH. Type style: Helvetica Extra Compressed. Horizontal scale: 300%. Baseline: Curved.
4. *H.* Type style: Helvetica Extra Compressed outlined. Horizontal scale: 400%.
   Holistic. Type style: Helvetica Ultra Compressed.
   HEALTH CENTER. Type style: Helvetica Condensed Light.

Applications

Logo. *Holistic.* Type style: Helvetica Condensed Black Oblique.
Health Center. Type style: Helvetica Condensed Black.
5. **Envelope.** (#10 business) *Logo.*
   Address. Type style: Helvetica Condensed. Size: 8 points. Interline: 10 points.
6. **Business Card.** (3.5x2) *Logo.*
   Tag line/Name. Type style: Helvetica Condensed Black. Size: 9 points. Interline: 11 points.
   Address. Type style: Helvetica Condensed. Size: 8 points. Interline: 11 points.
7. **Sign.** *Logo.*

1

HOLISTIC
HEALTH
CENTER

2

HOLISTIC
HEALTH
CENTER

3

HEALTH CENTER

4

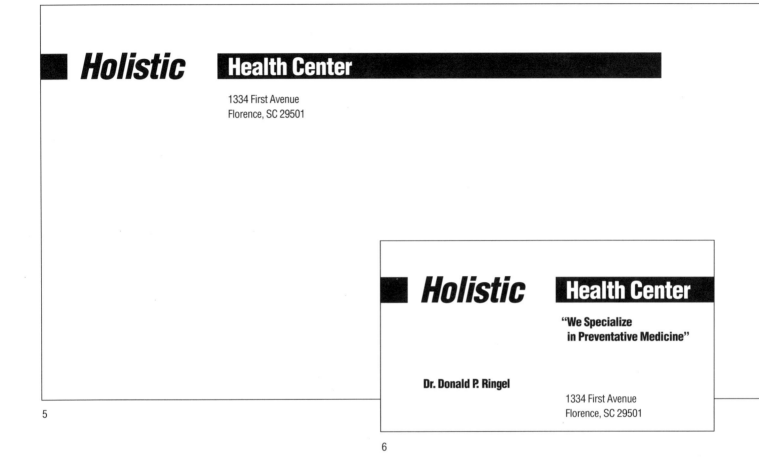

Holistic **Health Center**

1334 First Avenue
Florence, SC 29501

5

Holistic **Health Center**

**"We Specialize
in Preventative Medicine"**

Dr. Donald P. Ringel

1334 First Avenue
Florence, SC 29501

6

Holistic **Health Center**

**"We Specialize
in Preventative Medicine"**

7

The Body Shop fitness center shows how the use of expanded and condensed Helvetica Condensed Bold and Black can create a personal, strong and dynamic image.

Logos

1. ***The/Shop.*** Type style: Helvetica Condensed Oblique.
   BODY. Type style: Helvetica Extra Compressed.
2. ***The/Shop.*** Type style: Helvetica Condensed Light. Horizontal scale: 60%.
   BODY. Type style: Helvetica Ultra Compressed. Horizontal scale: 60%.
3. ***The Body Shop.*** Type style: Helvetica Condensed Bold Oblique.
4. ***the/shop.*** Type style: Helvetica Condensed Black Oblique.
   BODY. Type style: Helvetica Ultra Compressed outlined. Oblique: 20 degrees. Horizontal scale: 70%.

Applications

   Logo. *THE/SHOP.* Type style: Helvetica Condensed Black.
   BODY. Type style: Helvetica Extra Compressed. Horizontal scale: 150%. Baseline: Curved.

5. **Newspaper Ad.** (3x5) ***Logo.***
   Tag line. Type style: Helvetica Condensed Bold. Size: 18 points. Interline: 22 points.
   Services. Type style: Helvetica Condensed Black. Size: 14 points. Interline: 17 points.
   Address. Type style: Helvetica Condensed. Size: 13 points. Interline: 17 points.
   Phone. Type style: Helvetica Condensed Black. Size: 18 points.
6. **Business Card.** (2x3.5) ***Logo.***
   Tag line/Name. Type style: Helvetica Condensed Bold. Size: 10 points. Interline: 12 points.
   Address/Phone. Type style: Helvetica Condensed. Size: 9 points. Interline: 12 points.
7. **T-Shirt.** ***Logo.***

1

2

The Body Shop

3

4

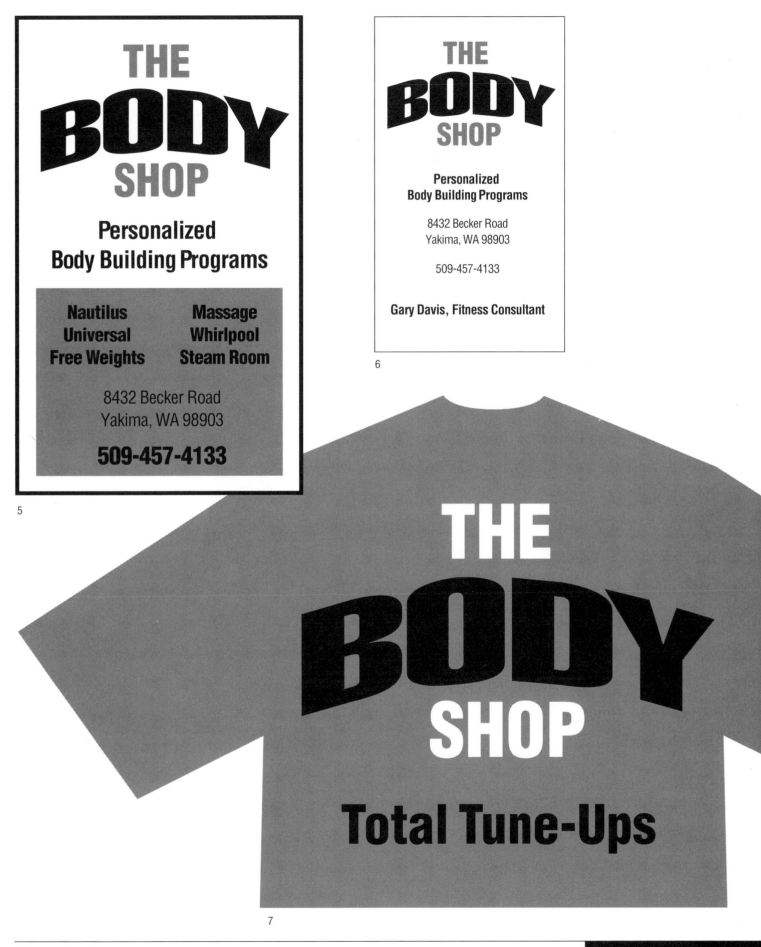

THE
BODY
SHOP

**Personalized
Body Building Programs**

Nautilus	**Massage**
Universal	**Whirlpool**
Free Weights	**Steam Room**

8432 Becker Road
Yakima, WA 98903

509-457-4133

5

THE
BODY
SHOP

**Personalized
Body Building Programs**

8432 Becker Road
Yakima, WA 98903

509-457-4133

Gary Davis, Fitness Consultant

6

THE
BODY
SHOP

Total Tune-Ups

7

The Top Notch tree service demonstrates the use of combining type effects such as outlined and condensed or expanded letters to produce a mechanical looking image for the business.

Logos

1. *t.* Type style: Helvetica Ultra Compressed outlined. Horizontal scale: 300%.
   top notch. Type style: Helvetica Condensed Black. Horizontal scale: 85%.
2. *T.* Type style: Helvetica Extra Compressed. Horizontal scale: 400%.
   top notch. Type style: Helvetica Ultra Compressed. Horizontal scale: 85%.
3. *top.* Type style: Helvetica Ultra Compressed. Horizontal scale: 300%.
   NOTCH. Type style: Helvetica Condensed Black.
4. *TOP.* Type style: Helvetica Condensed Light. Horizontal scale: 300%.
   notch. Type style: Helvetica Condensed Black Oblique. Horizontal scale: 85%.

Applications

Logo. *top.* Type style: Helvetica Ultra Compressed outlined.
notch. Type style: Helvetica Condensed Black. Horizontal scale: 85%.

5. **Newspaper Ad.** (5x6.5) *Logo.*
   Tag line/Phone. Type style: Helvetica Condensed Black. Size: 22 points. Interline: 27 points.
   Services/Address. Type style: Helvetica Condensed. Size: 18 points. Interline: 22 points.
6. **Business Card.** (2x3.5) *Logo.*
   Tag line/Phone. Type style: Helvetica Condensed Black. Size: 10 points. Interline: 12 points.
   Name. Type style: Helvetica Condensed Black. Size: 12 points.
   Address. Type style: Helvetica Condensed. Size: 10 points. Interline: 12 points.
7. **Truck.** *Logo.*

1

2

3

4

topnotch

Tree Trimming and Stump Removal

Year-Round
Citywide and Suburbs
Free Estimates

201-347-5561

72 Howe Street
Corley, NJ 07032

5

topnotch

**Tree Trimming
and Stump Removal**

Jim Clark, Owner

72 Howe Street
Corley, NJ 07032

201-347-5561

6

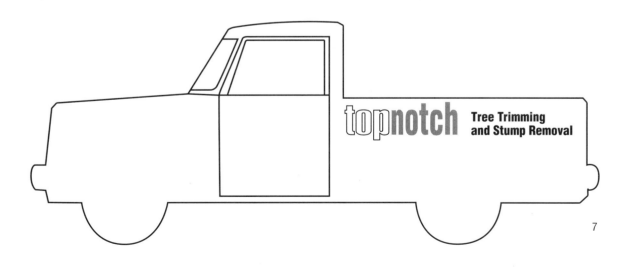

7

The use of centered alignment and capital letters produces a clean image, projecting the reliability and warm professionalism of the Holistic Health Center.

Logos

1. ***Holistic Health Center.*** Type style: Optima Bold.
2. ***Holistic Health Center.*** Type style: Optima.
3. ***HOLISTIC.*** Type style: Optima Bold. ***HEALTH CENTER.*** Type style: Optima.
4. ***H.*** Type style: Optima Bold. ***HOLISTIC HEALTH CENTER.*** Type style: Optima.
5. ***HOLISTIC.*** Type style: Optima Bold. ***HEALTH CENTER.*** Type style: Optima.

Applications

Logo. ***HOLISTIC HEALTH CENTER.*** Type style: Optima Bold.
6. **Outdoor Sign.** ***Logo.***
7. **Business Card.** (2x3.5) ***Logo.*** ***Tag line/Phone.*** Type style: Optima Bold. Size: 14 points. Interline: 17 points. ***Address/Name.*** Type style: Optima. Size: 10 points.
8. **Envelope.** (#10 business) ***Logo.*** ***Tag line.*** Type style: Optima Bold. Size: 13 points. Interline: 15 points. ***Address.*** Type style: Optima. Size: 10 points.

Holistic
Health Center

1

2

HOLISTIC
HEALTH CENTER

3

HOLISTIC
HEALTH
CENTER

4

HOLISTIC
EALTH CENTER

5

HOLISTIC
HEALTH CENTER

6

HOLISTIC
HEALTH CENTER

Specialized
Preventative Medicine

1334 First Ave., Florence, SC 29501

8

HOLISTIC
HEALTH CENTER

Specialized
Preventative Medicine

1334 First Ave., Florence, SC 29501

803-669-2121

Dr. Donald P. Ringel

7

These logos for Off the Cuff, which sells vintage evening wear, illustrate how Optima can be used with other graphics, such as the horizontal lines representing the cuff of a jacket, and the type as symbolic cuff links.

Logos

1. *Off the Cuff.* Type style: Optima.
2. *Off/Cuff.* Type style: Optima Bold Oblique.
   the. Type style: Optima Oblique.
3. *Off the Cuff.* Type style: Optima Oblique.
4. *Off the Cuff.* Type style: Optima Oblique.
5. *Off/Cuff.* Type style: Optima Bold.
   the. Type style: Optima.

Applications

Logo. *Off/Cuff.* Type style: Optima Bold Oblique.
the. Type style: Optima Oblique.

6. **Letterhead.** (8.5x11) *Logo.*
   Tag line. Type style: Optima Bold Oblique. Size: 12 points. Interline: 15 points.
   Address. Type style: Optima Oblique. Size: 10 points. Interline: 13 points.
   Phone. Type style: Optima Bold Oblique. Size: 10 points.
7. **Business Card.** (2x3.5) *Logo.*
   Tag line. Type style: Optima Bold Oblique. Size: 12 points. Interline: 15 points.
   Address/Title. Type style: Optima Oblique. Size: 10 points. Interline: 13 points.
   Phone/Name. Type style: Optima Bold Oblique. Size: 10 points.
8. **Price Tag.** (4.5x2) *Logo.*
   Information. Type style: Optima Bold Oblique. Size: 16 points. Interline: 20 points.

1

2

3

4

5

Off _the_
Cuff

Vintage Evening Wear
and Accessories

1104 Seneca Avenue
Norfolk, Virginia 23516
804/627-3681

Off _the_
Cuff

Vintage Evening Wear
and Accessories

1104 Seneca Avenue
Norfolk, Virginia 23516
804/627-3681

Blair Jamieson, Owner

7

Off _the_
Cuff

Style   Size
Code   Price

8

6

Optima's personal charm gives an image of confidence and honesty when applied to Anson C. Borst and Associates, a neighborhood law firm.

Logos

1. ***Anson C. Borst and Associates.*** Type style: Optima Bold.
2. ***AA.*** Type style: Optima Bold. Horizontal scale: 90%.
   Anson C. Borst and Associates. Type style: Optima. Horizontal scale: 90%.
3. ***Anson C. Borst and Associates.*** Type style: Optima.
4. ***a.*** Type style: Optima Bold Oblique.
   Anson C. Borst and Associates. Type style: Optima. Horizontal scale: 90%.
5. ***Anson C. Borst and Associates.*** Type style: Optima Oblique.

Applications

Logo. ***Anson C. Borst/Associates.*** Type style: Optima Bold.
and. Type style: Optima Oblique.
6. **Invoice.** (8.5x11) ***Logo.***
   Tag line/Address/Phone. Type style: Optima Oblique. Size: 9 points. Interline: 11 points.
   Information. Type style: Optima Bold. Size: 10 points. Interline: 14 points.
7. **Envelope.** (#10 business) ***Logo.***
   Address. Type style: Optima Oblique. Size: 9 points. Interline: 11 points.
8. **Business Card.** (3.5x2) ***Logo.***
   Tag line/Address/Phone. Type style: Optima Oblique. Size: 9 points. Interline: 11 points.
   Name. Type style: Optima Bold. Size: 11 points.

Anson C. Borst and Associates

1

2

Anson C. Borst and Associates

3

4

Anson C. Borst and Associates

5

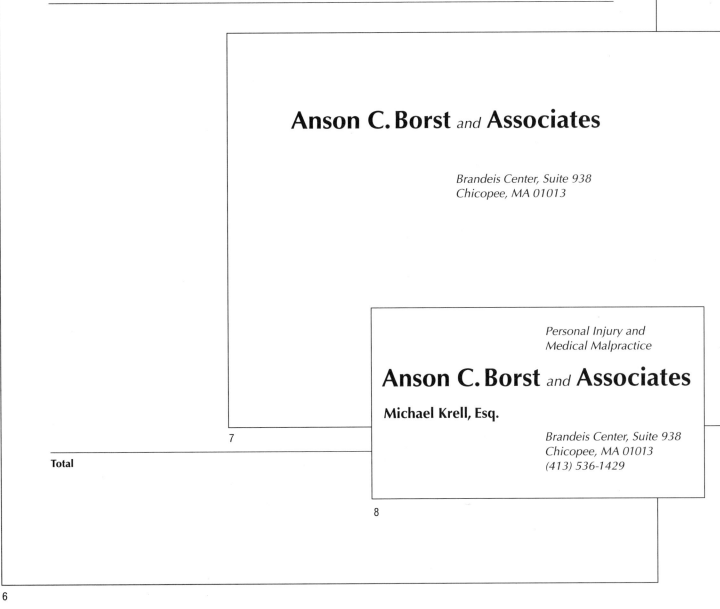

Personal Injury and
Medical Malpractice

Anson C. Borst *and* **Associates**

Brandeis Center, Suite 938
Chicopee, MA 01013
(413) 536-1429

Invoice

Date:
Client Number:
Matter Number:

7

Total

Anson C. Borst *and* **Associates**

Brandeis Center, Suite 938
Chicopee, MA 01013

Personal Injury and
Medical Malpractice

Anson C. Borst *and* **Associates**

Michael Krell, Esq.

Brandeis Center, Suite 938
Chicopee, MA 01013
(413) 536-1429

8

6

Borders, frames and rules are used with Optima to produce an inviting and reliable image for the Inwood Credit Union.

Logos

1. *INWOOD.* Type style: Optima Bold.
   Credit Union. Type style: Optima.
2. *INWOOD.* Type style: Optima Bold.
   CREDIT UNION. Type style: Optima.
3. *INWOOD/UNION.* Type style: Optima Bold.
   CREDIT. Type style: Optima Bold outlined.
4. *INWOOD.* Type style: Optima Bold Oblique.
   CREDIT UNION. Type style: Optima Oblique.
5. *Inwood.* Type style: Optima Bold.
   CREDIT UNION. Type style: Optima.

Applications

    Logo. *INWOOD.* Type style: Optima Bold.
    CREDIT UNION. Type style: Optima.
6. **Letterhead.** (8.5x11) *Logo.*
   Address. Type style: Optima. Size: 9 points.
7. **Business Card.** (3.5x2) *Logo.*
   Address. Type style: Optima. Size: 9 points.
   Name/Title. Type style: Optima Bold. Size: 11 points. Interline: 13 points.
8. **Passbook.** (6x4) *Logo.*
   Tag line/Address. Type style: Optima. Size: 12 points.
   Passbook. Type style: Optima Bold. Size: 36 points.

1

2

3

4

INWOOD

CREDIT
Inwood
UNION

5

INWOOD
CREDIT UNION

6452 Elm Avenue, Inwood, Indiana 47374 317-962-8254

INWOOD
CREDIT UNION

6452 Elm Avenue, Inwood, Indiana 47374 317-962-8254

Ira Ellman
Credit Representative

7

INWOOD
CREDIT UNION

"Celebrating 50 years of Personal Service to Our Members"

PASSBOOK

6452 Elm Avenue, Inwood, Indiana 47374 317-962-8254

6

8

Sky Wheels airport taxi service shows how Syntax Italic and outlined styles can be used to convey motion and flight.

Logos

1. *SkyWheels.* Type style: Syntax Ultra Black.
2. *Sky Wheels.* Type style: Syntax. Horizontal scale: 70%.
3. *SKY WHEELS.* Type style: Syntax Black. Horizontal scale: 75%.
4. *SKY.* Type style: Syntax Ultra Black outlined. Horizontal scale: 200%. *WHEELS.* Type style: Syntax Ultra Black.
5. *SKY.* Type style: Syntax Ultra Black outlined. Horizontal scale: 75%. *WHEELS.* Type style: Syntax Ultra Black. Horizontal scale: 300%.

Applications

Logo. SkyWheels. Type style: Syntax Black oblique.
6. **Newspaper Ad.** (2.5x3) *Logo.*
Phone. Type style: Syntax Italic. Size: 30 points.
Headline. Type style: Syntax Italic. Size: 14 points. Interline: 16 points.
Tag line. Type style: Syntax Black. Size: 8 points. Interline: 10 points.
Address. Type style: Syntax Black. Size: 8 points. Interline: 10 points.
7. **Envelope.** (#10 business) *Logo.*
Phone. Type style: Syntax Italic. Size: 29 points.
Tag line/Address. Type style: Syntax Italic. Size: 9 points. Interline: 11 points.
8. **Business Card.** (3.5x2) *Logo.*
Phone. Type style: Syntax Italic. Size: 41 points.
Tag line/Address. Type style: Syntax Italic. Size: 9 points. Interline: 11 points.
9. **Taxi.** *Logo.*

1

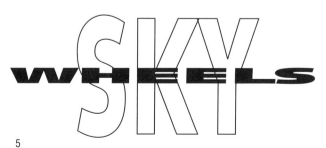

2

3

4

5

Special Airport Service
24-Hour Radio Dispatch

301-685-0692
SkyWheels

Special Airport Service
24-Hour Radio Dispatch

301-685-0692
SkyWheels

Costs Less Than Airport Shuttle
We Deliver On Time, Citywide

2749 Turner Ln.
Baltimore, MD.
21201

6

2749 Turner Ln.
Baltimore, MD.
21201

7

Special Airport Service
24-Hour Radio Dispatch

301-685-0692
SkyWheels

2749 Turner Ln.
Baltimore, MD.
21201

8

301-685-0692
SkyWheels

9

Scaletti's Italian restaurant is an example that emphasizes the contrast between the angular details, contrasting weights and subtle curves of Syntax.

Logos

1. *Scaletti's.* Type style: Syntax Italic.
2. *Scaletti's.* Type style: Syntax Black outlined.
3. *SCALETTI'S.* Type style: Syntax Bold.
4. *S.* Type style: Syntax Ultra Black. *Scaletti's.* Type style: Syntax Black.
5. *scaletti's.* Type style: Syntax Ultra Black.

Applications

Logo. *s.* Type style: Syntax Black. Horizontal scale: 250%.
scaletti's. Type style: Syntax Ultra Black.

6. **Menu.** (6.75x17) *Logo.*
Date. Type style: Syntax Ultra Black. Size: 26 points.
Menu. Type style: Syntax Ultra Black. Size: 56 points.

7. **Newspaper Ad.** (2.5x3) *Logo.*
Address/Phone. Type style: Syntax Ultra Black. Size: 10 points. Interline: 12 points.
Headline. Type style: Syntax Ultra Black. Size: 14 points. Interline: 15 points.
Features. Type style: Syntax. Size: 9 points. Interline: 13 points.

8. **Order Ticket.** (5x7) *Logo.*
Address/Phone. Type style: Syntax Ultra Black. Size: 10 points. Interline: 12 points.
Information. Type style: Syntax Ultra Black. Size: 9 points.

1

2

3

4

5

6

7

featuring italian specialties
private parties 15 to 50
valet parking
call for reservations now

quantity	item	cost
	subtotal	
	tax	
	total	

8

Down the Aisle wedding services logos reveal the subtle angular characteristics that help to create a strong personal quality in Syntax.

Logos

1. ***Down the Aisle.*** Type style: Syntax.
   A. Type style: Syntax Black outlined.
2. ***Down the Aisle.*** Type style: Syntax Black.
3. ***Down the Aisle.*** Type style: Syntax Black.
   ∞. Type style: Syntax.
4. ***Down the Aisle.*** Type style: Syntax.

Applications

   Logo. ***down the Aisle.*** Type style: Syntax Italic. Horizontal scale: 90%.
   A. Type style: Syntax Black slanted.
5. **Newspaper Ad.** (5x3) ***Logo.***
   Phone/Tag line. Type style: Syntax Bold. Size: 15 points.
   Services. Type style: Syntax Italic. Size: 12 points. Interline: 12 points.
   Address. Type style: Syntax Italic. Size: 11 points. Interline: 12 points.
6. **Business Card.** (3.5x2) ***Logo.***
   Name/Title. Type style: Syntax Italic. Size: 10 points. Interline: 12 points.
   Tag line/Address/Phone. Type style: Syntax Bold. Size: 10 points. Interline: 12 points.
7. **Van.** ***Logo.***

Down the /A\ isle

1

D o w n   t h e   A i s l e

2

Down
the
Aisle

3

Down
the
Aisle

4

312 W. Eastland
Parker, W. Virginia 26201

down the Aisle

complete wedding services

Limousines
Tuxedos
Photography
Bridal Registry
Invitations
Flowers
Gowns
Travel

304-472-4600

5

Rose Selkin
Wedding Consultant

down the Aisle

complete wedding services

312 W. Eastland
Parker, W. Virginia
26201

304-472-4600

6

down the Aisle

complete wedding services

304-472-4600

7

This example of Syntax shows how the large initial letters used in the Top Notch tree service logos can symbolically represent a tree.

Logos

1. *t.* Type style: Syntax Black. Horizontal scale: 85%.
   top notch. Type style: Syntax Black. Horizontal scale: 85%.
2. *top.* Type style: Syntax Black outlined.
   notch. Type style: Syntax Bold. Horizontal scale: 85%.
3. *top.* Type style: Syntax Black. Horizontal scale: 200%.
   NOTCH. Type style: Syntax Bold. Horizontal scale: 90%.
4. *TOP.* Type style: Syntax Black. Horizontal scale: 300%.
   notch. Type style: Syntax Italic.
5. *TOP.* Type style: Syntax Black. Horizontal scale: 300%.
   notch. Type style: Syntax Black.

Applications

Logo. *T.* Type style: Syntax Ultra Black. Horizontal scale: 400%.
top notch. Type style: Syntax Black.
6. **Business Card.** (3.5x2) *Logo.*
   Tag line. Type style: Syntax Bold. Size: 10 points.
   Address/Name. Type style: Syntax Bold. Size: 9 points.
   Phone. Type style: Syntax Ultra Black. Size: 20 points.
7. **Newspaper Ad.** (5x6.25) *Logo.*
   Tag line/Address. Type style: Syntax . Size: 14 points.
   Services. Type style: Syntax Ultra Black. Size: 18 points. Interline: 21 points.
   Phone. Type style: Syntax Black. Size: 29 points.
8. **Truck.**

1

2

3

4

5

tree trimming and stump removal

Top notch

year-round
citywide and suburbs
fully insured
free estimates

201/347-5561

72 howe st., corley, NJ 07032

tree trimming and stump removal

Top notch

jim clark, owner

201/347-5561

72 howe st., corley, NJ 07032

6

7

201/347-5561

Top notch

tree trimming and stump removal

8

Odilon, a fashionable boutique, displays the graphic distortions and effects that are possible with a type family like Syntax.

Logos

1. *O.* Type style: Syntax Black.
   ODILON. Type style: Syntax Italic.
2. *Odilon.* Type style: Syntax Black shadowed. Horizontal scale: 175%.
3. *Odilon.* Type style: Syntax Italic. Horizontal scale: 250%.
4. *ODILON.* Type style: Syntax Bold. Baseline: Curved.
5. *Odilon.* Type style: Syntax Black outlined and shadowed. Horizontal scale: 175%.

Applications

Logo. *Odilon.* Type style: Syntax Italic. Horizontal scale: 230%. Effect: Multiple.
6. **Shopping Bag.** *Logo.*
7. **Business Card.** (2x3.5) *Logo.*
   Tag line/Name/Phone. Type style: Syntax Ultra Black. Size: 10 points. Interline: 12 points.
   Title. Type style: Syntax. Size: 9 points.
   Address. Type style: Syntax Bold. Size: 9 points. Interline: 12 points.
8. **Price Tag.** (2x4.25) *Logo.*
   Tag line/Information. Type style: Syntax Ultra Black. Size: 10 points. Interline: 12 points.

1

2

3

ODILON

4

5

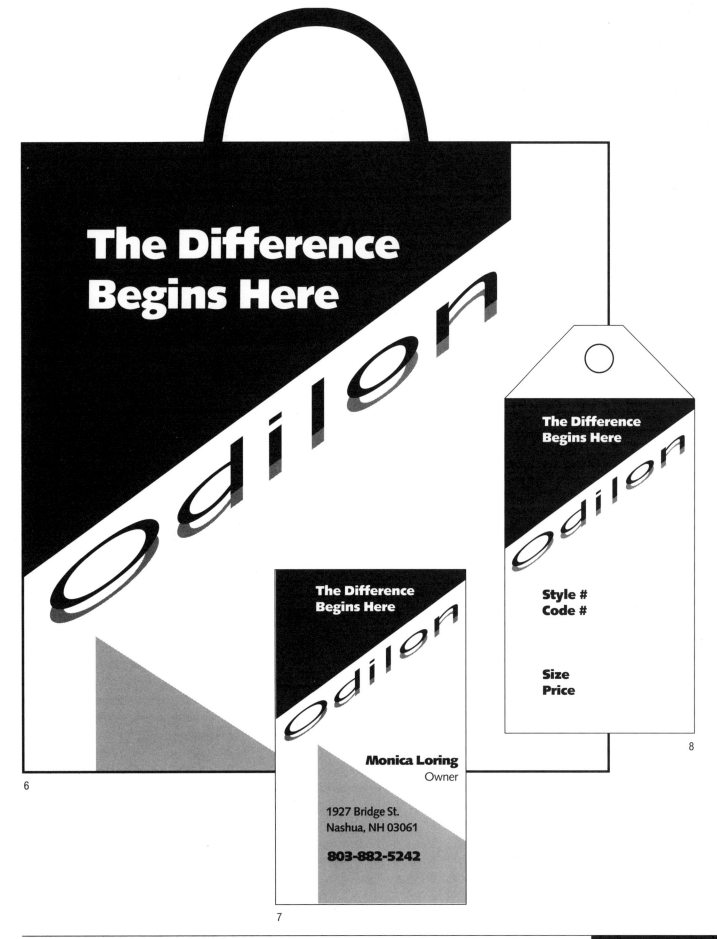

The Difference
Begins Here

odilon

The Difference
Begins Here

odilon

Style #
Code #

Size
Price

8

The Difference
Begins Here

odilon

Monica Loring
Owner

1927 Bridge St.
Nashua, NH 03061

803-882-5242

6

7

The Inwood Credit Union examples show how Times Roman creates an easy-to-read image that suggests reliability and trust.

Logos

1. ***INWOOD.*** Type style: Times Bold.
   CREDIT UNION. Type style: Times.
2. ***INWOOD/UNION.*** Type style: Times Bold.
   CREDIT. Type style: Times outlined.
3. ***CREDIT/UNION.*** Type style: Times Bold outlined.
   INWOOD. Type style: Times Bold Italic.
4. ***CREDIT/UNION.*** Type style: Times Bold.
   Inwood. Type style: Times Bold. Horizontal scale: 80%.

Applications

   Logo. *INWOOD.* Type style: Times Bold.
   CREDIT UNION. Type style: Times
5. **Envelope.** (#10 business) ***Logo.***
   Address. Type style: Times. Size: 10 points.
6. **Passbook.** (4x6) ***Logo.***
   Passbook. Type style: Times Bold. Size: 36 points.
   Address/Phone. Type style: Times. Size: 19 points.
7. **Business Card.** (3.5x2) ***Logo.***
   Name. Type style: Times Bold. Size: 13 points.
   Address/Phone. Type style: Times. Size: 11 points.

1

2

3

4

INWOOD
CREDIT UNION

6452 Elm Avenue, Inwood, IN 47374

5

INWOOD
CREDIT UNION

PASSBOOK

6452 Elm Avenue, Inwood, IN 47374 (317)962-8254

6

INWOOD
CREDIT UNION

Ira Ellman, Credit Representative

6452 Elm Avenue, Inwood, IN 47374 (317)962-8254

7

Norman's Heating and Cooling has an easy-to-read image produced using a mix of Times Roman styles.

Logos

1. **Norman's.** Type style: Times Bold Italic. **HEATING & COOLING, INC.** Type style: Times.
2. **Norman's.** Type style: Times Bold Italic. **HEATING & COOLING, INC.** Type style: Times Italic. Horizontal scale: 130%.
3. **norman's.** Type style: Times Bold. **HEATING & COOLING, INC.** Type style: Times.
4. **NORMAN'S.** Type style: Times Bold Italic. **HEATING & COOLING, INC.** Type style: Times Italic.
5. **Norman's.** Type style: Times Bold Italic. **HEATING & COOLING, INC.** Type style: Times Bold and Bold outlined.

Applications

Logo. Norman's. Type style: Times Bold. **HEATING & COOLING, INC.** Type style: Times Bold. Horizontal scale: 240%.

6. **Letterhead.** (8.5x11) **Logo.** **Tag line.** Type style: Times Bold. Size: 13 points. **Address/Phone.** Type style: Times. Size: 10 points. Interline: 12 points.
7. **Business Card.** (3.5x2) **Logo.** **Tag line.** Type style: Times Bold. Size: 13 points. **Address/Phone.** Type style: Times. Size: 10 points. Interline: 12 points.
8. **Ad.** (5x3) **Logo.** **Tag line/Phone.** Type style: Times Bold. Size: 16 points. **Services.** Type style: Times. Size: 12 points. Interline: 14 points. **Address.** Type style: Times. Size: 9 points.

1

2

3

4

5

1920 Russel Avenue, Orange, CA 92668
714-634-9564

1920 Russel Avenue, Orange, CA 92668
714-634-9564

7

We Service All Makes
No Extra Charge for Nights, Weekends or Holidays

714-634-9564

1920 Russel Avenue, Orange, CA 92668

6

8

Times Roman produces an easy-to-read image with a personal touch for Sky Wheel airport taxi.

Logos

1. *Sky Wheels.* Type style: Times Bold Italic.
2. *SKY WHEELS.* Type style: Times Bold. Horizontal scale: 75%.
3. *SKY.* Type style: Times Bold outlined. Horizontal scale: 200%.
   WHEELS. Type style: Times Bold.
4. *SKY.* Type style: Times Bold Italic outlined.
   WHEELS. Times Bold.
5. *Sky.* Type style: Times Bold Italic.
   WHEELS. Type style: Times Italic.

Applications

   Logo. S/W. Type style: Times Bold.
Sky Wheels. Type style: Times Bold Italic.

6. **Business Card.** (3.5x2) *Logo.*
   Tag line. Type style: Times. Size: 19 points.
   Phone. Type style: Times Bold. Size: 22 points.
   Services/Address. Type style: Times Bold. Size: 10 points. Interline: 12 points.
7. **Ad.** (5x6.25) *Logo.*
   Tag line. Type style: Times. Size: 31 points.
   Phone. Type style: Times Bold. Size: 33 points.
   Services. Type style: Times Bold. Size: 21 points. Interline: 24 points.
   Address. Type style: Times. Size: 15 points.
8. **Envelope.** (#10 business) *Logo.*
   Tag line. Type style: Times. Size: 14 points.
   Services/Address. Type style: Times. Size: 8 points. Interline: 11 points.

1

2

3

4

5

SkyWheels

Special Airport Service

301-685-0692

24-Hour Radio Dispatch
2749 Turner Lane, Baltimore, MD 21201

6

SkyWheels

Special Airport Service

301-685-0692

**24-Hour Radio Dispatch
Citywide
Fast Service
We Deliver On Time**

2749 Turner Lane, Baltimore, MD 21201

7

SkyWheels

Special Airport Service

24-Hour Radio Dispatch
2749 Turner Lane, Baltimore, MD 21201

8

Tigger Too is used to illustrate how Times Roman, reminiscent of children's books, adds personal charm to a toy shop's logo.

Logos

1. **TIGGER T.** Type style: Times Bold. Horizontal scale: 80%.
   OO. Type style: Times Bold. Horizontal scale: 300%.
2. **TT.** Type style: Times Bold Italic. Horizontal scale: 300%.
   TIGGER TOO. Type style: Times. Horizontal scale: 80%.
3. **TT.** Type style: Times Bold. Scale: Free form.
   Tigger Too. Type style: Times Italic.
4. **TT.** Type style: Times Bold. Horizontal scale: 500%.
   TIGGER TOO. Type style: Times. Horizontal scale: 80%.
5. **TIGGER TOO.** Type style: Times Bold. Scale: Free form.
   GG/OO. Type style: Times Bold. Scale: Free form.

Applications

Logo. **TT.** Type style: Times Bold.
Tigger Too. Type style: Times Bold.
6. **Ad.** (2.5x3) **Logo.**
   Tag line/ Services/Phone. Type style: Times Bold. Size: 13 points. Interline: 16 points.
   Address. Type style: Times. Size: 13 points. Interline: 16 points.
7. **Business Card.** (3.5x2) **Logo.**
   Tag line. Type style: Times Bold. Size: 9 points.
   Name/Address/Phone. Type style: Times. Size: 9 points. Interline: 11 points.
8. **Shopping Bag.** **Logo.**

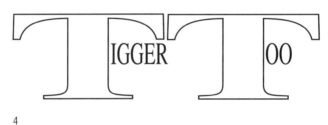

1

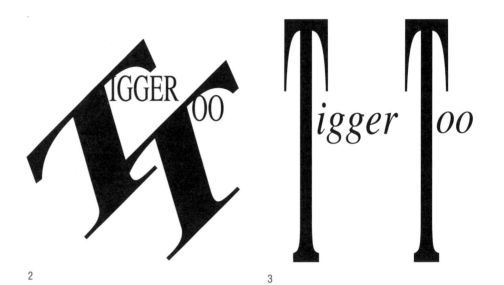

2

3

4

5

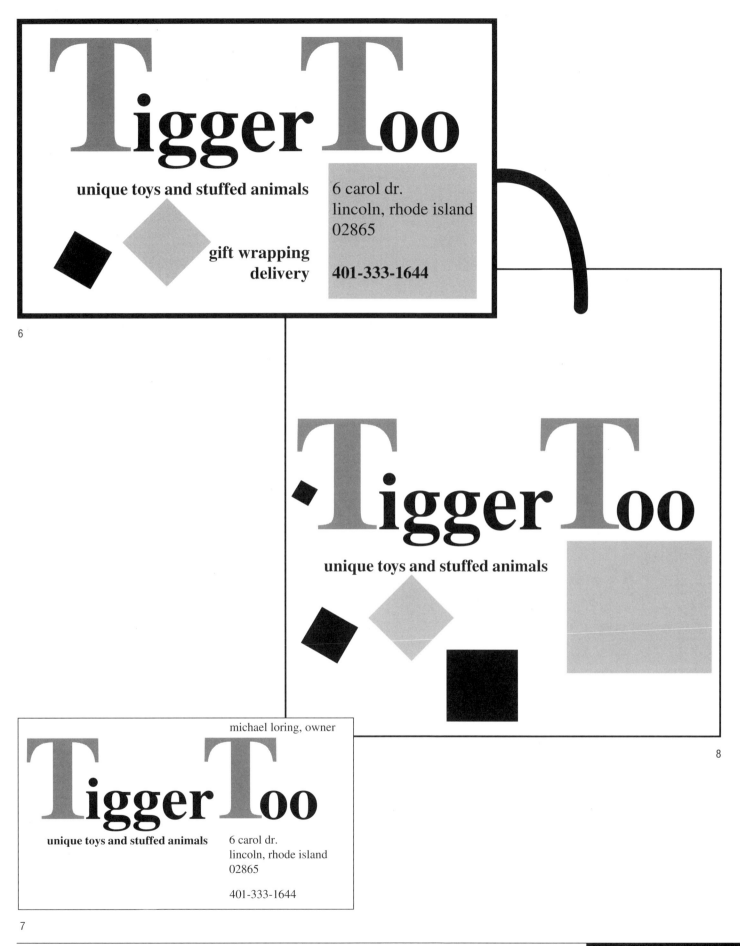

6

Tigger Too

unique toys and stuffed animals

6 carol dr.
lincoln, rhode island
02865

**gift wrapping
delivery**   **401-333-1644**

Tigger Too

unique toys and stuffed animals

8

michael loring, owner

Tigger Too

unique toys and stuffed animals   6 carol dr.
lincoln, rhode island
02865

401-333-1644

7

Times Roman and Italics are used for Down the Aisle wedding services logos to show how you can convey an image of reliability and trust using a readable type style.

Logos

1. *D.* Type style: Times outlined.
   Down the Aisle. Type style: Times Bold Italic.
2. *Down the Aisle.* Type style: Times Bold Italic.
3. *Down the Aisle.* Type style: Times. Horizontal scale: 85%.
4. *Down the Aisle.* Type style: Times.
5. *A.* Type style: Times outlined.
   Down the Aisle. Type style: Times Bold.

Applications

Logo. *A.* Type style: Times Bold.
down the Aisle. Type style: Times Italic. Horizontal scale: 85%.
6. **Ad.** (5x3) *Logo.*
   Tag line/Phone. Type style: Times Bold Italic. Size: 18 points.
   Services. Type style: Times Italic. Size: 14 points. Interline: 17 points.
   Address. Type style: Times Italic. Size: 10 points.
7. **Envelope.** (#10 business) *Logo.*
   Tag line. Type style: Times Bold Italic. Size: 12 points.
   Address. Type style: Times Italic. Size: 9 points. Interline: 11 points.
8. **Business Card.** (3.5x2) *Logo.*
   Tag line/Name/Phone. Type style: Times Bold Italic. Size: 12 points. Interline: 11 points.
   Address/Title. Type style: Times Italic. Size: 9 points. Interline: 11 points.

1

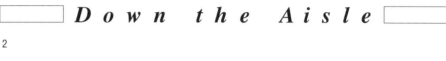

2

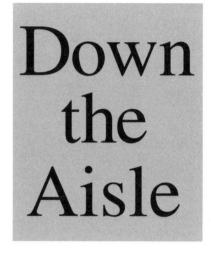

3

4

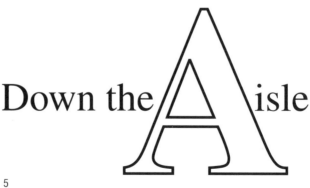

5

down the Aisle

Complete Wedding Services

Photography	*Gowns*
Bridal Registry	*Tuxedos*
Invitations	*Flowers*
Limousines	*Travel*

304/372-4600

312 W. Eastland Dr., Parker, WV 26201

6

down the Aisle

Complete Wedding Services

312 W. Eastland Dr.
Parker, WV 26201

7

down the Aisle

Complete Wedding Services

312 W. Eastland Dr.
Parker, WV 26201

304/372-4600

Rose Selkin
Wedding Consultant

8

Trump is used to create an image of old craft and integrity in these logos for the Hamlin Construction Co.

Logos

1. *hamlin.* Type style: Trump Bold. Horizontal scale: 90%.
   CONSTRUCTION CO. Type style: Trump. Horizontal scale: 80%.
2. *H.* Type style: Trump Bold outlined.
   HAMLIN. Type style: Trump Bold. Horizontal scale: 70%.
   CONSTRUCTION CO. Type style: Trump.
3. *HAMLIN.* Type style: Trump Italic.
   CONSTRUCTION CO. Type style: Trump.
4. *HAMLIN CONSTRUCTION CO.* Type style: Trump.
5. *hamlin.* Type style. Trump Bold. Horizontal scale: 80%.
   CONSTRUCTION COMPANY. Type style: Trump Italic. Horizontal scale: 70%.

Applications

Logo. hamlin. Type style: Trump Bold. *CONSTRUCTION CO.* Type style: Trump.

6. **Envelope.** (#10 business) *Logo.*
   Headline. Type style: Trump Bold. Size: 12 points.
   Address. Type style: Trump. Size: 11 points. Interline: 13 points.
7. **Newspaper Ad.** (4x5) *Logo.*
   Headline. Type style: Trump Bold. Size: 24 points.
   Tag line/Phone. Type style: Trump Bold. Size: 13 points. Interline: 18 points.
   Address. Type style: Trump. Size: 11 points. Interline: 14 points.
8. **Van.** *Logo.*
9. **Business Card.** (2x3.5) *Logo.*
   Headline. Type style: Trump Bold. Size: 12 points.
   Address/Title. Type style: Trump. Size: 11 points. Interline: 14 points.
   Name. Type style: Trump Bold. 13 points.

1

2

3

4

5

CONSTRUCTION CO.

hamlin

CONSTRUCTION CO.

Commercial/Residential

4256 Ogden Lane
Westlake, NJ 07007

6

---

hamlin

CONSTRUCTION CO.

Commercial/Residential

"One Call Does It All"
Free Estimates

4256 Ogden Lane
Westlake, NJ 07007

201-882-6044

7

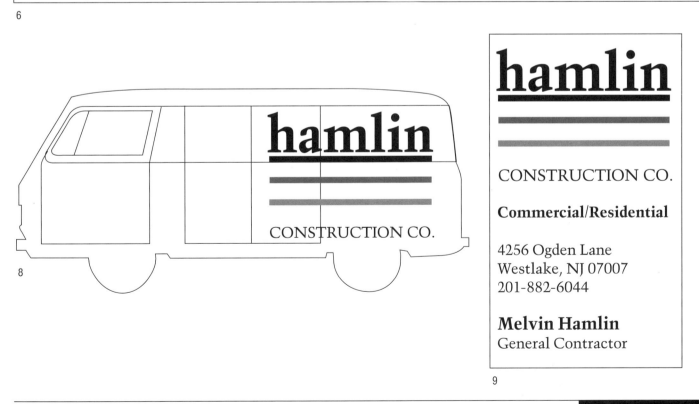

8

hamlin

CONSTRUCTION CO.

---

hamlin

CONSTRUCTION CO.

Commercial/Residential

4256 Ogden Lane
Westlake, NJ 07007
201-882-6044

Melvin Hamlin
General Contractor

9

Trump is the perfect type style for a business like Off the Cuff, which sells vintage evening wear. The logos also demonstrate the effective use of extreme horizontal expansion of the bold style.

Logos

1. *Off the Cuff.* Type style: Trump Italic.
2. *Off.* Type style: Trump Bold.
   the Cuff. Type style: Trump Italic oblique.
3. *OFF THE CUFF.* Type style: Trump Bold. Horizontal scale: 150%.
4. *OFF THE CUFF.* Type style: Trump Bold. Horizontal scale: 150%.
5. *OFF.* Type style. Trump Bold. Horizontal scale: 300%.
   THE/CUFF. Type style: Trump Bold.

Applications

   Logo. Off the Cuff. Type style: Trump Bold. Horizontal scale: 75%.
6. **Letterhead.** (8.5x11) *Tag line.*
   Type style: Trump Italic. Size: 12 points.
   Name. Type style: Trump Bold Italic. Size: 11 points. Horizontal scale: 75%.
   Address. Type style: Trump Italic. Size: 10 points. Horizontal scale: 75%.
7. **Envelope.** (#10 business) *Logo.*
   Tag line. Type style: Trump Italic. Size: 12 points. Horizontal scale: 75%.
   Address. Type style: Trump Italic. Size: 10 points. Horizontal scale: 75%.
8. **Business Card.** (3.5x2) *Logo.*
   Tag line. Type style: Trump. Size: 12 points. Horizontal scale: 75%.
   Name. Type style: Trump Bold Italic. Size: 12 points. Horizontal scale: 75%.
   Address. Type style: Trump Italic. Size: 10 points. Horizontal scale: 75%.
9. **Sales Slip.** (5x7) *Logo.*
   Tag line. Type style: Trump. Size: 12 points. Horizontal scale: 75%.
   Information. Type style: Trump Bold Italic. Size: 11 points. Horizontal scale: 75%.
   Address. Type style: Trump Italic. Size: 10 points. Horizontal scale: 75%.

Off the Cuff

1

2

3

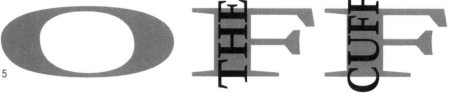

4

5

Off the Cuff

Vintage Evening Wear & Accessories

Blair Jamieson, Owner
1104 Seneca Ave., Norfolk, VA 23516 (804)627-3681

Off the Cuff

Vintage Evening Wear & Accessories

Blair Jamieson, Owner
1104 Seneca Ave., Norfolk, VA 23516 (804)627-3681

8

Off the Cuff

Vintage Evening Wear & Accessories

1104 Seneca Ave., Norfolk, VA 23516 (804)627-3681

7

6

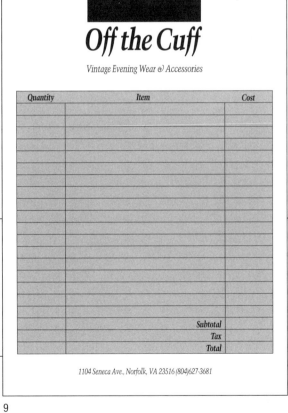

Off the Cuff

Vintage Evening Wear & Accessories

Quantity	Item	Cost
	Subtotal	
	Tax	
	Total	

1104 Seneca Ave., Norfolk, VA 23516 (804)627-3681

9

The moderate contrast between thin and thick strokes and the angled serifs of Trump and Trump Bold produces a look of integrity for the Inwood Credit Union.

Logos

1. *Credit Union.* Type style: Trump. *INWOOD.* Type style: Trump.
2. *INWOOD.* Type style: Trump Bold. *CREDIT UNION.* Type style: Trump.
3. *INWOOD.* Type style: Trump Bold. *CREDIT.* Type style: Trump outlined. *UNION.* Type style: Trump.
4. *CREDIT.* Type style: Trump outlined. *INWOOD.* Type style: Trump Bold Italic. *UNION.* Type style: Trump.
5. *Inwood.* Type style: Trump Bold. *CREDIT.* Type style: Trump outlined. *UNION.* Type style: Trump.

Applications

　Logo. Inwood. Type style: Trump Bold. Horizontal scale: 75%. *CREDIT UNION.* Type style: Trump Bold.
6. **Letterhead.** (8.5x11) *Logo. Address/Phone.* Type style: Trump. Size: 12 points. Interline: 18 points.
7. **Business Card.** (3.5x2) *Logo. Address/Phone.* Type style: Trump. Size: 10 points. Interline: 13 points. *Name.* Type style: Trump Bold. Size: 11 points.
8. **Passbook.** (6x4) *Logo. Tag line/Address.* Type style: Trump. Size: 13 points. Horizontal scale: 75%. *Passbook.* Type style: Trump Bold. Size: 24 points.

1

2

3

4

5

CREDIT Inwood UNION

6452 Elm Avenue, Inwood, Indiana 47474

417/962-8254

CREDIT Inwood UNION

6452 Elm Avenue, Inwood, Indiana 47474

417/962-8254

Ira Ellman, Credit Representative

7

CREDIT Inwood UNION

"Celebrating 50 Years of Personal Service to Our Membership"

PASSBOOK

6452 Elm Avenue, Inwood, Indiana 47474 417/962-8254

8

6

The logo used in these applications takes advantage of graphic line elements and a reversed background to enhance the image.

Logos

1. *ARIEL.* Type style: Trump Bold. Horizontal scale: 110%.
   ARIEL STRING QUARTET. Type style: Trump Bold. Horizontal scale: 130%.
2. *ARIEL.* Type style: Trump Bold.
   STRING QUARTET. Type style: Trump Bold. Horizontal scale: 80%.
3. *ARIEL.* Type style: Trump.
   STRING. Type style: Trump Bold. Horizontal scale: 170%.
   QUARTET. Type style: Trump. Horizontal scale: 70%.
4. *ARIEL.* Type style: Trump.
   STRING. Type style: Trump Bold. Horizontal scale: 170%.
   QUARTET. Type style: Trump. Horizontal scale: 80%.
5. *Ariel String Quartet.* Type style: Trump.

Applications

Logo. *Ariel String Quartet.* Type style: Trump Bold.
6. **Letterhead.** (8.5x11) *Logo.*
   Name. Type style: Trump Bold. Size: 10 points.
   Address/Phone. Type style: Trump. Size: 9 points. Interline: 16 points.
7. **Business Card.** (2x3.5) *Logo.*
   Name. Type style: Trump. Size: 10 points.
   Address. Type style: Trump Bold. Size: 8 points. Interline: 11 points.
8. **Envelope.** (#10 business) *Logo.*
   Name. Type style: Trump Bold. Size: 10 points.
   Address. Type style: Trump. Size: 9 points.

ARIEL
ARIEL STRING QUARTET

1

2

3

4

5

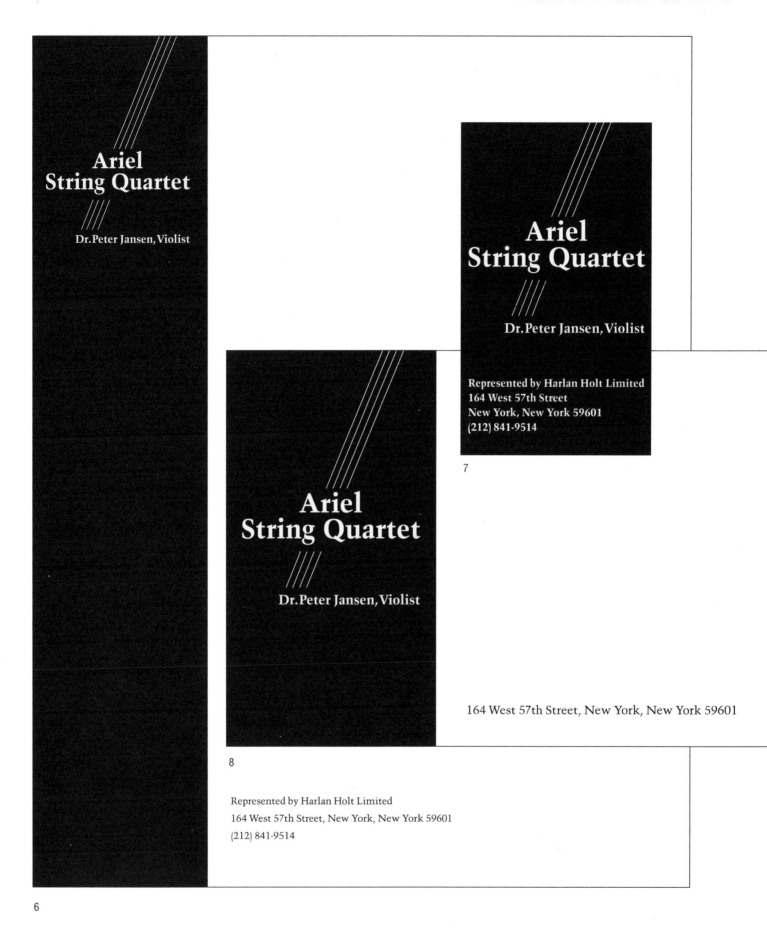

**Ariel
String Quartet**

Dr. Peter Jansen, Violist

**Ariel
String Quartet**

Dr. Peter Jansen, Violist

Represented by Harlan Holt Limited
164 West 57th Street
New York, New York 59601
(212) 841-9514

7

**Ariel
String Quartet**

Dr. Peter Jansen, Violist

164 West 57th Street, New York, New York 59601

8

Represented by Harlan Holt Limited
164 West 57th Street, New York, New York 59601
(212) 841-9514

6

Norman's Heating and Cooling, Inc. is a good example of how you can effectively use Trump in no-frills simple centered alignment compositions.

Logos

1. ***Norman's.*** Type style: Trump Bold. ***HEATING & COOLING, INC.*** Type style: Trump Bold. Horizontal scale: 150%.
2. ***NORMAN'S.*** Type style: Trump Bold. ***HEATING & COOLING, INC.*** Type style: Trump.
3. ***Norman's.*** Type style: Trump Bold Italic. ***HEATING & COOLING, INC.*** Type style: Trump Italic.
4. ***NORMAN'S.*** Type style: Trump Bold Italic.
   HEATING & COOLING, INC. Type style: Trump Italic.
5. ***Norman's.*** Type style: Trump Bold. Horizontal scale: 85%.
   HEATING & COOLING, INC. Type style: Trump Bold. Horizontal scale: 80%.

Applications

Logo. ***NORMAN'S.*** Type style: Trump Bold.
HEATING & COOLING, INC. Type style: Trump. Horizontal scale: 130%.

6. **Job Estimate.** (8.5x11) ***Logo.***
   Services/Address. Type style: Trump. Size: 8 points.
   Phone. Type style: Trump Bold. Size: 11 points.
   Information. Type style: Trump Bold. Size: 10 points. Interline: 14 points.
7. **Business Card.** (3.5x2) ***Logo.***
   Services/Address. Type style: Trump. Size: 10 points.
   Phone. Type style: Trump Bold. Size: 13 points.
8. **Newspaper Ad.** (2.5x3) ***Logo.***
   Headline/Phone. Type style: Trump Bold. Size: 12 points. Interline: 16 points.
   Services/Address. Type style: Trump. Size: 8 points. Interline: 10 points.

1

2

3

4

5

NORMAN'S
HEATING & COOLING CO.
Sales • Service • Installation • Cleaning

714-634-9564

ESTIMATE
1920 Russel Avenue, Orange, CA 92668

DATE:
CLIENT:
ADDRESS:
PHONE NUMBER:
JOB NUMBER:

LABOR:

NORMAN'S
HEATING & COOLING CO.
Sales • Service • Installation • Cleaning

714-634-9564

1920 Russel Avenue, Orange, CA 92668

7

NORMAN'S
HEATING & COOLING CO.

SALES
SERVICE
INSTALLATION
CLEANING

We Service All Makes

No Extra Charge
for Nights, Weekends, or Holidays

714-634-9564
1920 Russel Avenue, Orange, CA 92668

8

MATERIALS:

SUBTOTAL:
TAX:
TOTAL:

6

About the Collection

I have selected examples of works produced by professional designers that extend the concept of type moods into actual practice. **The collection is represented by ads, logos, newsletters, business forms, book covers, newspaper section pages and posters produced by professional designers, illustrators and photographers.** You'll be inspired by the ideas presented in this part of the book. Although type styles alone can produce a mood, as you have seen in Part 2, the use of illustrations will greatly enhance a mood. I want you to look very carefully at the relationships of type and how the illustrations support the mood as you look through this part of the book.

Trendy

The designers who produced these examples shared a common goal. They produced clean contemporary images that project a progressive and experimental quality.

Notice the integration of the *r* and *M* in the **Rochester Monotype logo *(page 128, figure 1)*.** This combination of Bodoni Italic and a modified Helvetica type style create a trendy mood. This mixture of type styles suggests a progressive future with a foundation in the past.

Nostalgic

Notice the consistent centered orientation of the compositions. It was only after the works were selected that I became aware of the fact that each example contained a plant form. Each illustration is a different style of drawing yet the mood in each example is consistent in producing a nostalgic look.

The Progressive Architecture invitation is a double invitation *(page 129, figure 1)*. The illustration reads as a furniture setting when the Progressive Architecture type is at the top and as a rocket ship when the invitation is flipped and NASA News type is at the top.

Traditional

These examples show us that almost any serifed type style can be used to give a personable look to the page.

A *popular* use of traditional mood typography is exhibited in the **Pier 1 advertisement *(page 130, figure 2)*.** In this case the designer used Century Schoolbook type style to add a warm touch to a simple composition of colorful window shades.

Classic

Discover type style subtleties such as the elegant figure-ground relationships of the letters that appear in these examples.

The **Elegant Fare** logo places particular importance on the quality of the letterforms themselves to achieve a distinctive tasteful image.

Playful

You'll discover how you can mix different type families to create a playful mood in the **Pizzazz** logo *(page 132, figure 2)*. Much of the playfulness of the mood is created by the unexpected interaction of different types. This example appears intuitive although it is designed in a controlled manner to provide a cohesive logo.

Aggressive

The attention-getting characteristic and the imperative image created in these examples typifies the aggressive mood produced by condensed bold type styles.

Notice how the designers use contrasting elements in most of the examples *(page 133, figures 2,3,4)*. The chalk letters and the use of serif type adds a personal touch that softens the harsh gothic letters.

Friendly

The friendly charm of the Optima type styles is demonstrated in three different types of applications *(page 134, figures 1,2,3)*. Optima Bold is used to catch the viewer's eye in the **CINDERS** poster. Also, notice the the figure-ground relationship of the type and the illustration on the poster. The **NUTRITION** textbook cover makes good use of the Optima letters that relate to similar shapes found in the illustration. The **BUFFUM** logo demonstrates the versatility of combining drawn illustrations and letterforms to make a friendly logo for a dentist.

Flair

Creating a flair mood often requires a bit of experimentation and the use of contrasting elements. The **MUTUAL INTEREST** newsletter presents financial information with a flair through the use of colors, shapes and photographs *(page 135, figure 1)*. They are intuitively organized on the page to contrast the grid used for the text.

The **Bailey OFFICE PRODUCTS** logo was constructed with actual paper clips and photographed to create the logo *(page 135, figure 2)*.

Informative

The primary function of typography is to inform. So why are some type families and type styles more informative than others? The most informative type families are designed for easy reading, without decoration or stylistic distortions. Serif type families like Times Roman and Century Schoolbook, and sans serifs like Helvetica and Univers are good examples of informative type.

The **Sun Newspaper Food Section** page uses a simple six-column grid *(page 136, figure 3)*. The grid is interrupted by placing a four-column full-color illustration behind with two partial columns in the center of the page. The layout incorporates a mix of Franklin Gothic and Century Schoolbook to present the material to the reader.

Sophisticated

The examples used to illustrate this mood show how dramatically the composition, and the illustrations' style and content influence the viewer's perception of what is sophisticated.

The **JUILLIARD** poster is a beautiful combination of the type style Novarese and pictorial illustration *(page 137, figure 2)*. Look for the simple composition, linear elements and shapes used to produce a

1. **Rochester Monotype Logo.**
   M. Type style: Helvetica (modified). *r.*
   Type style: Bodoni Italic. *Rochester.*
   Type style: Bodoni Italic. *Monotype.*
   Type style: Helvetica Black. Designers:
   Cynthia Hummel, John Dunn. Art
   Director: John Dunn. Client: Dunn &
   Rice Design.

2. **Mike Akins Logo.**
   Type style: Helvetica. Designer: Mike
   Akins. Art Directors: Mike Akins, Marc
   Connelly, Glen Bach. Client: Mike Akins
   Graphic Design.

3. **M'OTTO REDDOT Logo.**
   M'OTTO. Type style: Custom. *REDDOT.*
   Type style: Futura Bold. Designer: Glen
   Yonezawa. Art Director: Mark Dellplain.
   Client: M'otto Reddot.

4. **Kubas Fax Form.**
   Transmittal. Type style: Eurostyle.
   Address. Type style: Futura. *Fax.* Type
   style: Custom. Size: 8½ x 11. Designer:
   George Kubas II. Client: George Kubas II
   Design Associates, Inc. Copyright,
   George Kubas II Design Associates, Inc.

Rochester **Monotype**

1

m. ak+ns !

2

M'OTTO

R E D D O T

3

4

Nostalgic

1. **Progressive Architecture Invitation.**
   Type style: Bodoni Bold. Designer: Michael Bierut. Size: 5½x11 Client: International Design Center Purpose: Double invitation for two programs at the International Design Center. © Michael Beirut.

2. **Wyngate Business Park.**
   Type style: Race. Size: 5 x 7. Designer: Lynda Transou. Art Director: Madelyn Miller. Illustrator: Sue Ellen Brown. Client: Cambridge Properties. Purpose: Direct mail pieces from Cambridge Properties to advertise Wyngate Business Park.

3. **Fresh Produce Business Card.**
   Fresh Produce. Type style: Vendom Condensed. *Studio.* Type style: Johnston Railway Medium. *Text.* Type Style: Metro Medium. Size: 2 x 3½. Designer: Pamela & Thomas Gecan & Diana McPeak. Client: Fresh Produce Studio.

1

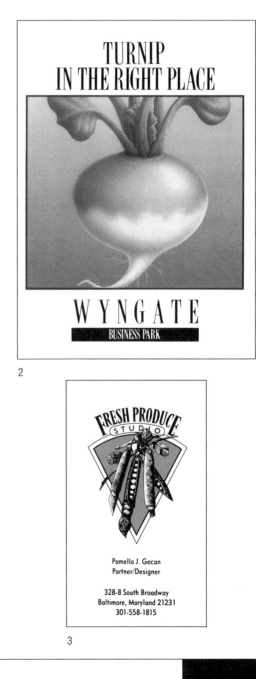

2

3

1. **Kids 'n Action Logo.**
   Type style: Futura Black. Designer: Tom Horton. Art Director: John Bricker. Client: Kids 'n Action, children's clothing store. © Kids 'n Action. Credit: Gensler and Associates/Architects.

2. **PIZZAZZ Logo.**
   P. Type style: Triumvirate Ultra Compressed. *i.* Type style: Caslon 540. *z.* Type style: Univers Extra Bold. *z.* Type style: Century Bold Italic. *a.* Type style: Futura Extra Bold. *z.* Type style: Triumvirate Ultra Compressed. *z.* Type style: Novarese. Designer: Richard Nelson, Kiku Obata & Co. Client: John

   Burroughs School. © Kiku Obata & Co., Rich Nelson–Designer.

3. **Mike Salisbury Request Form.**
   Type style: Futura. Size: 8½ x 11. Designer: Cindy Luck. Art Director: Mike Salisbury. Client: Mike Salisbury Communications.

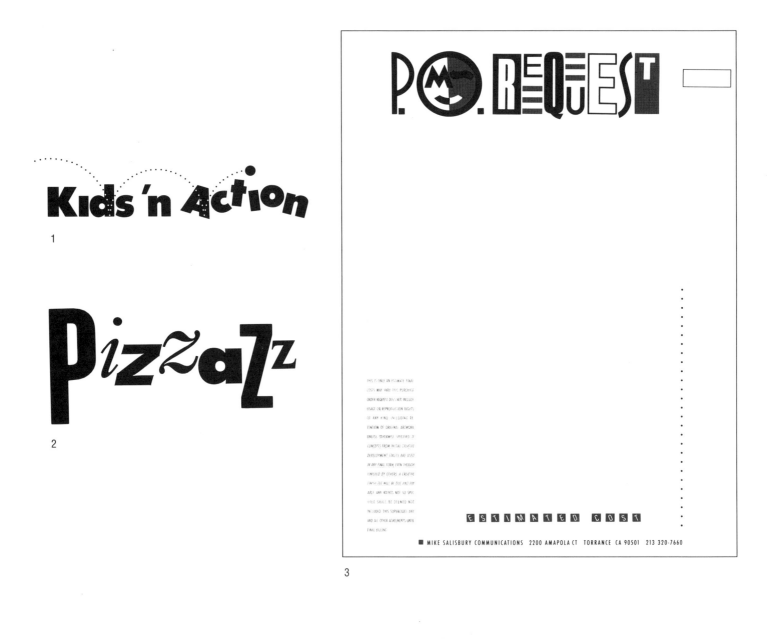

1

2

3

Aggressive

1. **Miles Davis Special Section Logo.**
Type style: Futura Extra Bold Condensed.
Designer/Art Director: Richard Leeds.
Client: Keyboard Magazine. ©1987
Richard Leeds Design.

2. **Chalkboard: Alumni Magazine Logo.**
Type style: Standard Extra Bold
Condensed. Designer: Paul Brown.
Client: Indiana University School of
Education.

3. **Skyline Newsletter.**
Skyline. Type style: Helvetica
Compressed Black. ***Heads/Subheads/
Text.*** Type style: Bodini Bold.
Designer/Art Director: Massimo Vignelli.
Client: Institute for Architecture & Urban
Studies.

4. **Boys Club Ad.**
Type style: Futura Extra Bold
Condensed. Size: 17¼ x 25½.
Designer/Art Director: Wayne Gibson,
The Martin Agency. Illustrator: Jerry
Torchia. Client: The Boy's Club.

1

2

3

LIKE MANY FATHERS, JAMES' DAD SHOWED HIM HOW TO SHOOT A GUN. HE WAS COMMITTING SUICIDE AT THE TIME.

This is a true story we recently faced at the Boys Club. So, if you think this is just a place where kids go to play basketball, think again.

And remember that when you support the Boys Club, you're also encouraging things like cultural appreciation, health education, job training, and counseling for boys in need of emotional support.

To learn how you can support these efforts, call 359-5250.

BOYS CLUBS OF RICHMOND

4

1. **Cinders: Poster.**
   CINDERS. Type style: Optima.
   Information. Type style: Optima. Size: 11x17. Designer: William Innes. Art Director/Typographer: Rhonda Taggart. Client: Drake University Theatre.
   © Graphic Design at Drake University.

2. **Nutrition Textbook Cover.**
   NUTRITION. Type style: Optima. Size: 8x10⅝. Designer: Marc Christianson. Illustrator: Pamela Noftsinger. Client: Wm. C. Brown Publishing. © Wm. C. Brown & Pamela Noftsinger.

3. **Buffum Logo.**
   BUFFUM. Type style: Optima (modified). Designer: Tim Celeski. Client: Kathryn Buffum D.D.S. © 1988 Tim Celeski, Tim Celeski Studios.

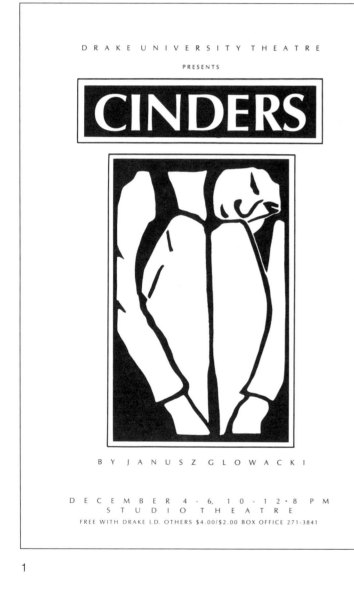

1

2

3

1. **Mutual Interest Newsletter.**
Mutual. Type style: Bodoni. ***Interest.***
Type style: Univers 67. ***News and…***
Type style: Bodoni Bold. ***Heads.*** Type
style: Bodoni Poster. ***Subheads.*** Type
style: Bodoni Bold. ***Text.*** Type style:
Futura. Size: 9x12. Designer: Tom
Kienberger. Client: The Pacific Mutual
Building.

2. **Bailey Office Products Logo.**
Bailey. Type style: Created by bending
paper clips into letter shapes then
photographing. ***OFFICE PRODUCTS.***
Type style: Palatino. Designer: Joe
Krawczyk. Client: Bailey Office Products.
© Krawczyk Design, Inc. 1989.

3. **Storyboards Logo.**
STORYBOARDS. Type style: Sigi.
Designer: Bob Dinetz/Petrula Vrontikis.
Art Director: Petrula Vrontikis. Client:
Storyboard Inc. (Agents for Storyboard
artists.)

1

2

3

1. **Newspaper Society Promotional Poster.**
Type style: Times Roman. Size: 21½ x 28.
Designer: Milton Glaser. Client: Society of
Newspaper Design.
2. **Mithun Partners Logo.**
Type style: Times Roman. Designer:
Hornall Anderson–Seattle. Client: Mithun
Partners, Inc. (Architecture planning and
interior design.)

3. **Sun Newspaper Food Section.**
The Sun. Type style: Century
Schoolbook. *Food.* Type style: Century
Book Ultra Condensed. *Holiday
recipes.* Type style: Century Old Style
Italic. *Your.* Type style: Franklin Gothic
Demi. *A Sampler.* Type style: Franklin
Gothic Book. *Text.* Type style: Century

Schoolbook. Size: 13¾ x 23. Designer:
Joni Levy Liberman. Art Director:
Mitchell J. Hayes. Client: Sun Publishing
Co. © The Sun Publishing Company.

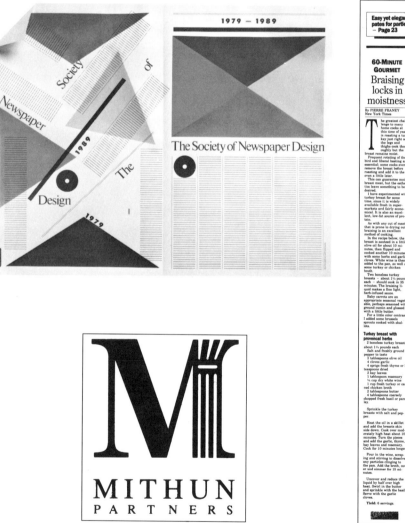

1

2

3

Sophisticated

1. **Manchester String Quartet Poster.**
   Type style: Garamond. Size: 22½ x 37.
   Designer/Illustrator: Peter Good. Client:
   The Merck Co. Foundation.
2. **Juilliard Promotional Poster.**
   Type style: Novarese. Size: 27 x 36.
   Designer: Milton Glaser. Client: Juilliard
   School.

3. **Ligature Magazine Cover.**
   D. Type style: Carnase Text. *ar*. Type
   style: Goudy. *G.* Type style: Cursirium.
   E. Type style: Futura. *Ligature.* Type
   style: Goudy. Size: 11 x 13½. Designer:
   Jason Calfo. Art Director: Tom Carnase.
   Client: World Typeface Center.

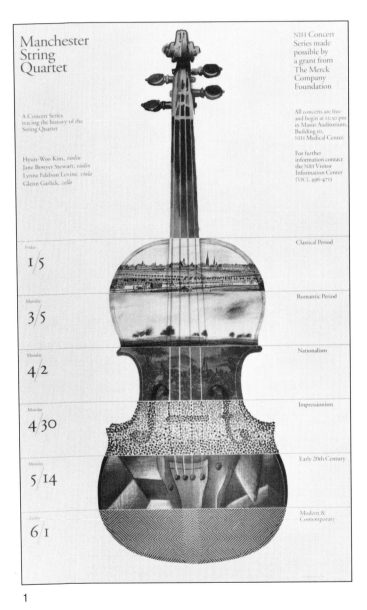

1

2

3

Ascender. Stroke of a lowercase letter that extends above the meanline.

Alignment. Horizontal and vertical positioning of elements in relation to each other.

Baseline. Guideline that capitals and the lowercase letters (not including the descenders) rest on.

Bold. Type style with thicker strokes than a text-weight font.

Cap height. Height of a capital letter.

Character. A letter, number or punctuation mark in a font or type style.

Character count. Number of characters in a specified text.

Condensed. Letter with a horizontal width that is narrower than normal.

Counter. Inner space (negative space) defined by the strokes of a given character.

Descender. Stroke of a lowercase letter that extends below the baseline.

Display type. Large letters used for headlines.

Em. A measurement traditionally defined as a square of the type size (example: 12x12 points).

En. Measurement that is traditionally half of an Em (example: 6x12 points).

Expanded. Letter with a horizontal width that is wider than normal.

Face. Part of the letter (positive) represented by the stroke(s).

Fit. Relationship between letters.

Flush. (Left or Right) Even alignment on one side of a text column.

Font. (See Type style)

Headline. First level of importance in a printed communication.

Horizontal scale. Mechanical adjustment to the width of a character or word that produces a condensed or expanded effect.

Interletter space. Space between letters.

Interline space. (Leading) Space between lines of type. A measurement from baseline to baseline that includes the type size.

Interword space. Space between words.

Italic. Type style with calligraphic characteristics that slants to the right.

Justified. Even alignment on both sides of a column of text.

Kerning. Adjustment that reduces space between two characters.

Leading. (See Interline space)

Legibility. The degree to which a type style is judged to be readable.

Letterform. Characteristics that make a letter unique from other letters.

Logo. (Logotype) A word used as a trademark.

Lowercase. Used to distinguish small letters from capitals.

Mean line. Guideline that marks the top of the lowercase letters.

Measure. Length of a line of type.

Modern. Roman type style with extreme contrast between thick and thin strokes.

Oblique. Slanted version of a regular type style (font).

Old Style. Roman type style with moderate thick to thin strokes, bracketed serifs, and a calligraphic influence.

Pica. A unit of measure in type. Six picas equals approximately one inch.

Point. (Printers) A unit of measure in type. Twelve points equals one pica. Seventy-two points equals approximately one inch.

Point. (Computer) A unit of measure in type. Seventy-two points equals exactly one inch.

Ragged. Type set with regular units of interword space that produce lines of different length.

Reverse type. Light colored letters set on a dark background.

River. Objectionable visual effect produced by excessive interword spacing or inadequate interline space that causes the eye to move vertically through the text.

Sans serif. Type styles without serifs.

Serif. Element at the end of a stroke that looks like a "foot."

Subhead. Secondary level of importance in a printed communication.

Tag line. Descriptive copy that may accompany a trademark.

Text. Main body of a printed page.

Transitional. Roman type style with characteristics of both Old Style and Modern designs.

Tracking. Spacing adjustment that affects the interletter and interword space.

Typeface. (See Type style).

Type family. Complete set of type styles including light, text, bold, expanded, condensed, italics and others.

Type style. (Typeface or Font) Complete set of alphabetic characters, upper and lowercase letters, punctuation marks and numerals of like style.

Type styling. The typographic modifications made to the original letters and their spacing relationships.

Type size. A measurement taken from just above the top of the ascender to just below the bottom of the descender.

Unit system. System of measurement used to determine all interletter and interword spacing.

Uppercase. Used to distinguish capitals from small letters.

Weight. Relative visual lightness or heaviness of a type style.

x-height. Height of the lowercase letters without the ascenders and descenders.